Children's Concepts of Gender

Margaret Jean Intons-Peterson
Indiana University

ABLEX PUBLISHING CORPORATION
NORWOOD, NEW JERSEY

LIBRARY OF CONGRESS
Library of Congress Cataloging-in-Publication Data

Intons-Peterson, Margaret Jean.
  Children's concepts of gender / Margaret Jean Intons-Peterson.
    p.   cm.
  Bibliography: p.
  Includes index.
  ISBN 0-89391-515-7
  1. Sex roles in children.   I. Title.
HQ784.S45I58   1988
305.3—dc19   88-4117
                                                                  CIP

ABLEX Publishing Corporation
355 Chestnut Street
Norwood, New Jersey 07648

Reprinted by permission of the Leyden University Library.

Table of Contents

*With fond regards for all their inspiration and support,
I gratefully dedicate this book to my husband, Lloyd,
and to our children.*

Four-year-old boy's drawing of a girl

Same four-year-old boy's drawing of a boy

CHAPTER 1

Girls and Boys:
Who and What Are They?

3-year-old: This one's a girl because she has red eyes.

Adult experimenter: (Pointing to the other drawing.) And what about this person?

Same child: Can't you tell? That one's a boy, of course. He has red eyes and no hair.

What does it mean to be a girl? A boy? How do children learn to distinguish between girls and boys? Do they learn first that they are a girl or a boy and then that others can be divided into two sexes? Or is it the other way around? Do they learn that there are two sexes before they learn that they belong to one of these groups? How do they learn what is expected of boys and girls? Of women and men? Do their views change with age? These questions are not only fascinating, they are central to human development: They address the child's emerging knowledge of gender roles and sexuality, as well as the child's developing sense of self, both as an individual and as a member of her or his culture.

What is "gender?" We use the term to refer to a whole complex of social beliefs, attitudes, behaviors, occupations, activities, and the like that are typically associated with females or with males in a given society. We use "gender" to designate the cultural, social, and psychological variations attributed to the two sexes and "sex" to refer to biological differences. Why the distinction, since sex may be the foundation on which the scaffolding of gender is constructed? We make the distinction, and emphasize gender over sex for a number of reasons. One is that we assign gender on the basis of what we perceive—what we see, hear, feel, and comprehend. In most contacts with other people, we typically do not see external genitalia, the overt

1

physical evidence of a person's biological sex, just as we do not usually know, with certainty, a person's exact sex-determining chromosomal pattern. Rather, we infer the biological information from the person's appearance, activities, and other aspects of what we call gender. We may, as adults, use secondary sexual characteristics, such as breasts, hip width, or facial hair to infer the biological sexual status of a person, but such inferences do not provide a satisfactory basis for correctly attributing sex for at least two reasons. The first is that, as we shall see, young children do *not* use these cues to distinguish the sexes (McConaghy, 1979). The second is that the variations in secondary sexual characteristics are so vast that these cues would be imperfect indicators. Some women have as little obvious breast development or as narrow hips as many men. Some women have facial hair. By contrast, some men have substantial breast development, wide hips, or minimal facial hair. It would be difficult to establish absolute standards for any of these secondary sexual characteristics that would invariably afford accurate gender identification of clothed individuals.

Another reason for using gender rather than sex as our basic referent to the distinctions between females and males is that social-cultural-psychological conventions associated with gender may override biological information. Consider, for example, the transsexuals who "pass" as the other sex even though they have not had genital surgery. Or genetic females or males who, following an early misidentification of their ambiguous external genitalia, have been successfully raised as members of the other sex (Money & Erhardt, 1972). For these reasons, then, we prefer the term gender.

Why are gender concepts societally critical? They serve a procreational purpose, of course, but their significance extends beyond a desire to perpetuate the species. Gender distinctions surely pervade most contacts between males and females, even when these distinctions are not motivated by sexual desire. One reason, sociologists tell us, is that gender functions as a "master" role. A "master" role is a central or major classifier of people within a culture. Concepts of gender, then, are used to divide individuals into two groups, the female and the male, and this distinction appears to be pancultural. Additionally, concepts of gender reflect beliefs about the two sexes. These concepts thus shape expectations for each sex; they fashion gender attitudes as surely as a potter molds clay. These concepts do more than govern perceptions of self; they direct self-expectations, comparisons of self with others of both sexes; they channel our attention to our environment, focusing on certain gender-related information, at the expense of others. Gender concepts govern perceptions of self and of others; they also mold or form perceptions of others. Our gender concepts, like other concepts we have, are magnets for attracting us to relevant information and away from irrelevant, potentially disconcerting information. Consider an avid chess or bridge player. This person will respond with alacrity to sophisticated information about the game, while ignoring other aspects of the environment. Similarly, a died-in-the-wool Republication or Democrat may listen to the speeches of candidates of the "right" persuasion, while deliberately avoiding speeches given by opponents. In other words, our concepts play a direct role in managing our contacts with what goes on around us, and this is as true with concepts about gender as with concepts about other aspects of our world.

Gender concepts permit the partitioning of our environments into various classifications or categories, which, regardless of the impact of these classifications, function to reduce the different kinds of stimuli, objects, beliefs, attitudes, and so forth, with which we deal in the course of our daily lives. These partitions divide one's world into the male and female, a stratification that invites differential treatment of the two categories.

Concepts of gender permeate our language (consider what a man says to the gas station attendant when he wants the attendant to fill the tank of a beloved possession, his car). They pervade our institutions, creating alternative forms for female and male versions of the same job classifications, such as waitress and waiter. Within the workplace, the knowledge of the sex that dominates occupations is often so pronounced that when the other sex becomes a member of the occupation, the language explicitly notes the exception, as with lady doctor, male nurse, male secretary, and lady plumber. Concepts of gender also influence our laws by creating predispositions about what is and is not appropriate behavior for the two sexes: Women are supposed to be better at caring for children; hence, child custody should be awarded to them, given no contraindicating evidence. Indeed, concepts about gender and their behavioral correlates are so pervasive in our culture that they even dictate such a seemingly trivial matter as the way our clothes button.

Other examples also illustrate the importance—and the salience—of gender attribution. The first question asked about a newborn usually is about its sex (Intons-Peterson & Reddel, 1984). Newspaper and other birth announcements proclaim the baby's sex. Indeed, lack of knowledge about a baby's sex makes adults noticeably uncomfortable (Seavey, Katz, & Zalk, 1975). Most impressive of all is the amazing proficiency with which preschool children identify gender. Thompson (1975) found that, on the average, 24-month-olds correctly identified the gender of 76% of pictured women and men; 30-month-olds identified 83%; and 36-month-olds identified 90%. Clearly, gender attribution is an important component of human organization. Gender does indeed play a master role in our society. The intriguing question is, therefore, how does it acquire its controlling significance?

This question is not new, of course. Many have speculated about the origins of the concept of gender, just as many have sought persuasive experimental evidence. Both the theories and the evidence are considered in subsequent chapters. For our purpose here, it is important to note that these past efforts have been valuable, for they have illuminated incomplete views and misconceptions about gender along with accurate perspectives.

Some of the theories have been largely disconfirmed by experimental evidence, but it is important to know what has not been explanatorily useful, just as it is helpful to understand the areas of promise. Among the best-known, oldest, and most tenacious theories are those of Sigmund Freud. His ideas have been perpetuated by numerous disciples, many of whom propounded their own modified theories, and by popularizers in various disciplines. Perhaps because of their longevity, many researchers have tried to experimentally test Freudian models (often called "psychoanalytic" or "psychodynamic" models). We now know, for example, that children do not always identify with or imitate the same-sex parent and that young children do not attach much importance to differences between the external genitalia of the two sexes, two suppositions central to psychoanalytic models. Their disconfirmation persuaded numerous psychological researchers to turn to other explanations. In addition, traditional psychoanalytic views imply that young children with only one parent would have disturbed, probably immature gender concepts compared to those of children with two parents. The research, although fraught with methodological problems and ambiguous results, typically does not support this view (see chapters in Lamb, 1976).

These examples illustrate how misconceptions can be used to eliminate potential origins of gender concepts, thereby channeling the search toward more productive possibilities. Review of the research literature discloses still other useful ideas. Parents are by no means the only source of information about gender roles. Peers, teachers, the media, and the rest of the child's world convey information which may establish or influence knowledge of and attitudes about gender roles.

Schools, whether intentionally or unintentionally, transmit ideas about gender (Chafetz, 1974). In the United States, the school hierarchy typically has male authority figures (principals) and female teachers. Although teachers often deny treating girls and boys differently and may have no intention of doing so, some evidence suggests that they may affirm gender-role differences by bestowing more positive and negative attention on boys than on girls. On the positive side, they call on boys more often than on girls; they recognize boys' creativity more than girls'; and they praise boys' efforts more than girls' (Brophy & Good, 1974; Cherry, 1975). Teachers also give more negative attention to boys than to girls, commenting on objectionable behavior, and the like (Good, Sikes, & Brophy, 1973; Huston, 1983; Serbin, O'Leary, Kent, & Tonick, 1973; Stake & Katz, 1982.) Both positive and negative attention affords public recognition to the children, of course, and may be interpreted by both girls and boys as indications that boys' achievements are more important, more valuable than those of girls.

Peers, too, use both positive and negative reinforcement to control behavior (Langlois & Downs, 1980). Boys are more likely to be teased than girls if they engage in activities considered by their peers to be gender-inappropriate. Indeed, boys who are called "sissies" when they play with girls or what their peers consider "girls' toys" usually change their ways quickly. In contrast, boys who play with "boys' toys" are encouraged by the acceptance of their activities. The effectiveness of peer pressure as a molder of perceptions about gender roles is well-illustrated by the film, *Men's Lives* produced by Josh Hanig and Will Roberts in 1974 (New Day Films). This film describes how social expectations constrain the gender roles of males as they grow from childhood to maturity.

Various forms of the media also contribute to the development of concepts about gender. Books, newspapers, magazines, film, television all depict the two sexes in different ways (Brabant, 1976; Cassata, 1983; Courtney & Whipple, 1983; Friedman, 1977; Frueh & McGhee, 1975; McArthur & Eisen, 1976; McGhee & Frueh, 1980; Murray, 1981; Potkay, Potkay, Boynton, & Klingbeil, 1982; St. Peter, 1979; Sternglanz & Serbin, 1974; and Weitzman, Eifler, Hokada, & Ross, 1972). At the risk of severely oversimplifying the standard results, I summarize them briefly by noting that girls and women are often absent. If they appear, they tend to be portrayed as passive onlookers. Boys and men have the active, exciting, decision-making roles. They engage in many different activities, in startling contrast to the limited roles assigned to women. Both print and audiovisual forms of the media present these stereotypes and do so with such regularity that it seems inevitable that they will influence perceptions of gender roles. But is this true? Are children and adults really affected by the media or do they discount media portrayals as fiction, unrelated to real life? It now appears that exposure may have lasting effects. For example, after children have read stereotyped books, they are more likely to want to play with stereotyped than nonstereotyped toys (Atkin, 1975; Frey & Ruble, 1981). In other work, children reverted to assigning a male name to a doctor and a female name to a nurse after seeing a film which showed a female doctor with a female name and a male nurse with a male name (Cordua, McGraw, & Drabman, 1979).

It seems, then, that constant bombardment by certain stereotypic gender roles leaves its mark. This mark may hone, chisel, or otherwise fashion gender concepts as they become increasingly differentiated. But the mark does not enlighten us about the *origins* of concepts about gender, for children show clear gender-related preferences by about two years of age. Toddler girls prefer to play with toys and dolls, to dress up, and to dance. Toddler boys prefer to play with transportation toys or blocks, to actively manipulate objects, and to play with items forbidden by their parents (Fagot, 1974, 1978; Fein, Johnson, Kosson, Stork, & Wasserman, 1975; Smith & Daglish, 1977). We know that children do not necessarily use the same cues to identify gender that adults use: Adults, not children, use genitalia and secondary sex characteristics (Kessler & McKenna, 1978; McConaghy, 1979; Thompson & Bentler, 1971). Thus, this research warns us that parents may not be the only determiners of their children's gender knowledge and that the gender cues of adult experimenters may not be the most functional indicators of gender for children.

We also need to be aware of accurate conceptions about children's gender information and the gaps in this knowledge. We know, for example, that children can identify the sex of pictured adults at a very early age—when they are as young as 24 months (Thompson, 1975), although we do not know the exact cues they use to do so. We have some information about children's views of the gender roles (e.g., Carter & Patterson, 1982; and Williams, Bennett, & Best, 1975). For example, Carter and Patterson found that children's knowledge of sex-role stereotypes for toys, adult occupations, and conventional table manners increased with age (the subjects were kindergartners through eighth graders), as did beliefs that gender role stereotypes and associated social conventions are flexible and culturally influenced. Even so, we do not yet know the origins or the developmental sequence typically followed by these views.

As the discerning reader will have noticed by now, we have talked about different kinds of knowledge about gender. We assume that the most fundamental is the knowledge of one's own sex, or what is often termed "gender identity." This knowledge is possessed by some two-year-olds, and by many two-and-a-half-year-olds (Fagot, 1985; Thompson, 1975). In addition, there is the awareness that gender tends to remain constant over time (often called gender stability or temporal gender constancy). This concept appears somewhat later than gender identity, between ages four and five, according to the above authors, as well as others. Two other important concepts are the notions of gender motive (the awareness that gender typically cannot change even if one wants it to do so) and gender constancy (knowledge that gender is invariant across situation, changes in attire, activities, and the like). The concept has also been called situational gender constancy. These concepts are acquired at about the same time as, or slightly later than that of gender motive (again, refer to the above-listed authors).

In addition to the classifications described above, all of which refer to notions of the consistency and reliability of an individual's maintaining a particular sex-gender affiliation across time and situations, we all learn other associations with gender. We acquire attitudes about activities, physical characteristics, personality traits, occupations, and attitudes that are stereotypically associated with each gender. In short, we acquire a host of beliefs about lifestyle attributes that distinguish between the sexes, or what we will label, for want of a more encompassing, descriptive term, gender roles (also called, somewhat inappropriately, sex roles).

Children provide many examples of the acquisition of gender role attributes, or gender typing (also called sex typing). By the time they are two-and-a-half years of age, children are often able to assign gender-related objects and activities (Blakemore, LaRue, & Olejnik, 1979; Fagot, 1985; Kuhn, Nash, & Brucken, 1978; Thompson, 1975). By the age of three, children accurately classify, by gender, activities, interests, and occupations (Edelbrock, & Sugawara, 1978; Falkender, 1980; Flerx, Fidler, & Rogers, 1976; Huston, 1983; Marantz & Mansfield, 1977; Masters & Wilkinson, 1976; Schau, Kahn, Diepold, & Cherry, 1980). Attributions of personality traits to females and males emerge somewhat later, between ages five and eleven (Best, Williams, Cloud, Davis, Robertson, Edwards, Giles, & Fowles, 1977; Williams, Bennett, & Best, 1975).

These various conceptions of gender have support and must be retained to identify, as precisely as possible, the particular variants of gender information at hand. Nonetheless, we need an omnibus term, a collective term to encompass this great constellation of gender-related information. We will use "gender concept" to refer to the overarching organization of gender-affiliated information. For a detailed consideration of the many ways of categorizing conceptualizations about gender, I refer the interested reader to Huston (1985).

Intrigued by the issues of the development of awareness of gender concepts in young children and attracted by their pivotal importance, my students and I began in 1980 what we thought was a limited research program. We first conducted an extensive review of the research literature and of theories of gender development. Chapter 2 summarizes the research, and Chapter 3 evaluates the theories. These efforts led to the formulation of our own model and to a series of experimental tests of the model. As so often happens with research programs, we found that the answers of each experiment raised exciting new questions. Thus, our efforts became a long-lasting, tantalizing, and ultimately rewarding quest, one that continues still. At this point, however, the broad outlines of how and what children learn about gender seem clear to us. This book describes those outlines and our tentative model for explaining gender acquisition.

Our initial model, like most others, is a product of previous work. To explain its origins and its rationale, I need to identify some of the notions that were instrumental to its generation.

Our central notion is that gender concepts are formed in the same way that other concepts are formed. We proposed that children acquire knowledge about gender in the same way that they acquire other knowledge. Some of the time they imitate the behavior of a like-sex model. If they are rewarded for this behavior, perhaps by being told they are "good boys" or "good girls," they are likely to continue the behavior—and to continue copying the model. If they imitate an other-sex model, they are likely to be discouraged by hearing that they did not act like a "boy" or a "girl." While the children may not understand what the adult means by acting like a girl or a boy, the child certainly is able to recognize attention, approval, and disapproval, and to behave accordingly. As these experiences accumulate, children learn to label themselves as girls or boys, just as they learn their names, and they develop a cognitive conceptualization (network) of the kinds of behaviors (attitudes, expectations, etc.) associated with being a girl or a boy, in addition to a conceptualization of the behaviors of the other sex. These developing concepts then may guide the child just as effectively as imitation and reinforcement.

At about age five to seven, children learn that objects in the world are relatively constant, bar some kind of accident. Thus, a red ball remains the same red ball, even if the paint chips off, unless it is reduced to bits by a lawnmower (even then it can be considered, in toto, as the parts of a ball). They learn that they have blue (brown, gray) eyes and that they will have the same color eyes throughout their lives. They become aware, then, of the relative permanence, constancy, and invariance of objects and some personal characteristics. They become aware that gender remains relatively constant over one's lifetime and that it remains constant in different situations. This knowledge is part of their gender concept.

By the time they are seven to ten years of age, their gender concepts include information about secondary sex characteristics and genitalia. Most of the information about characteristics, attitudes, behaviors, activities, occupations, and traits typically associated with each sex constitute what we call *cultural gender concepts*. These concepts represent the stereotypic view held by their society for each sex. We propose further that children develop a cultural gender concept for each sex. That is, children of both sexes learn what is usually associated with femaleness and what is usually associated with maleness in their society. We then faced a dilemma. Is one cultural gender concept developed faster than the other? Specifically, is the male gender concept acquired more rapidly than the female one, because of the preeminence accorded males in the United States? Several lines of research indicated that this might be the case. Williams and Best (1982) report that, in their cross-cultural research, male concepts develop earlier than female ones, and Kessler and McKenna (1978) found that whenever a penis was present their adult subjects were likely to say the picture was of a male regardless of other characteristics, such as breasts. This work led us to hypothesize that a male concept will be acquired earlier than a female one and that a male concept would be used as the system for classifying individuals. If people conform to the male concept, they are male; if they do not conform, they are female. As it turned out, our data were not consistent with this view, and we modified the final model described in Chapter 9.

In addition to the cultural gender concepts which code gender stereotypic information, we posit that children include gender-related items in their self- or personal concepts. Thus, the children learn their name, their eye color, their hair color, and their sex. They may include some aspects of their cultural gender concepts into their personal ones, depending on their experiences. Thus, if children think that most members of their sex are witty and that they, themselves, are witty, they may incorporate being witty into their personal gender schema, whereas others, who do not associate wittiness with either most members of their sex or with themselves, would not be expected to incorporate wittiness into their personal gender concept.

It is the self or personal concept that determines the extent to which children behave in gender-stereotypic ways. It is the self-concept that underlies the tremendous variation in adherence to stereotypic gender roles. Presumably, most or all people learn the cultural gender concepts of their society; they differ in their self concepts.

Because our primary interest was in the acquisition and contents of gender concepts, we focused primarily on young children as our research participants. In some cases, adults were tested as well.

Before summarizing the plan of the book, a few words are in order about our term "concept." This term is admittedly vague, but we use it in the sense of an organized, coherent, but independent set of features which collectively define the concept.

Most of this book is devoted to tests of the model described above. We begin by briefly describing some associated research (Chapter 2) and by theories of children's concepts of gender (Chapter 3). Then we consider the cues that young children use to identify gender (Chapters 4 and 5), children's concepts of the constancy of gender (Chapter 6), the contents of children's gender concepts (Chapter 7), and the relation between perceived gender roles and adjustment (Chapter 8), before drawing conclusions (Chapter 9).

Printed by permission of the children's mother.

CHAPTER 2

Sex, Gender, and Their Interaction

As we go about our daily lives, we assume that every human being is either a male or a female...Not even with biologically "mixed" individuals do we conclude that they are neither female nor male...(for)...in everyday life ultimately some criteria can (and will) be found by which each one is placed in one of two mutually exclusive categories...But consider a list of items that differentiate females from males. There are none that *always and without exception* are true of only one gender. (Kessler & McKenna, 1978, p. 1.).

As Kessler and McKenna (1978) suggest, we regularly divide people into the two mutually exclusive classes, male and female. Our birth certificates carry one or the other label. So do our driver's licenses and other identification cards. When filling out forms that ask for sex we are to check one of two alternatives. Society seems determined to impose this tidy dichotomy on its citizens, although the rationale and the necessity of doing so are rarely considered. How often does one see or hear a justification for this practice, for its utility? Some uses spring quickly to mind, such as the identification of people. But aren't there other means of identification? Other, more precise ways of distinguishing one person from others? These questions do not indicate an antagonism toward this societal practice, but rather a perplexity at the failure to question, defend, or explain it. The practice seems to have become so commonplace that its effectiveness, accuracy, and even purpose are often uncritically, unquestioningly accepted.

For practical purposes, most individuals, even young children, easily assign people to one sex or the other. The intriguing query is how do they make these assignments? What cues are used? How are the cues combined? What weights are given to specific cues? If, as Kessler and McKenna contend in the quotation that headed this chapter, no single cue or characteristic is

Figure 2.1   Child playing.

a perfect predictor of sex, we may use the cues probabilistically, perhaps relying more on some cues than on others. Consider, for example, the problem of identifying the gender of the child shown in Figure 2.1. This blond, straight-haired preschooler wears jeans, a T-shirt, and sneakers. The clothes really aren't much help, but if we think girls are more likely than boys to have blond hair, we are likely to conclude that the child is a girl. If we think that boys are more likely than girls to wear jeans, T-shirts, and sneakers and to have straight hair, we may conclude that the child is a boy.

Are these cues actually considered? Are probabilities or weights of the cues taken into account in some, perhaps nonconscious, way? For example, with the child in Figure 2.1, if hair color has greater weight for identifying gender than clothes, we will decide that the child is a girl. But do hair color plus hair length override clothing cues? Answers to these questions about how people are assigned to the two gender classes typically involve biological and cultural-social-societal characteristics. Unfortunately, neither the biological nor the cultural-social-societal classes infallibly separates persons in two gender categories. Gender classification is not as simple as it may seem. Let us consider some biological and some cultural-social-psychological cues that might serve to differentiate between the sexes.

Biological and Cultural-Social-Psychological Gender Markers

We begin with biology, an area which is often thought to be clear and unambiguous. Perhaps the best place to start is with sexually-reproducing "lower" animals. Two standard assumptions about the biological determination of sex are that the sex of the organism is determined by its heredity at the time of conception and that the animal's sex will remain unchanged throughout its life (except for surgical and pharmacological intervention). We expect these assumptions to hold for all animals who reproduce sexually, including, of course, map turtles and coral reef fish. Is the sex of map and of painted turtles (*Graptemys ouachitensils* and *Graptemys pseudogeographica*) determined at the time of conception? Not necessarily. Its sex is largely determined by the temperature of the water in which the egg was incubated. When the water is relatively warm, say between 24° and 27°C, most hatchlings are male; whereas when the water temperature is either colder, say 20°C, or warmer, 31°C or above, most hatchlings are female. This pattern cannot be explained by differential, prehatching mortality rates, because almost all of the eggs hatched in experiments in both a laboratory setting and in a wild habitat (Bull & Vogt, 1979). Moreover, some other turtles, (*Chelonia mydas*) show the same effect (Morreale, Ruiz, Spotila, & Standora, 1982).

Does the sex of coral reef fish (*Anthias squamipinnis*) remain unchanged throughout its life? Not necessarily. If a dominant fish of either sex dies or leaves the school, the dominant fish of the other sex will change. Moreover, there is almost perfect, one-for-one replacement, (Fricke & Fricke, 1977; Moyer & Nakazano, 1978; Shapiro, 1980). Change from female to male also may be induced in other coral reef fish, the saddleback wrasse (Thalassoma duperray), by visual stimulation from smaller fish of the same species (Ross, Losey, & Diamond, 1983). Further, some small basses (genus Hypoplectrus) are simultaneously hermaphroditic. That is, these fish produce eggs and sperm at the same time. More examples exist (Warner, 1984), but these few make the point that biology cannot always be used to invariantly and infallibly assign lower animals to two gender classes.

The same is true for the human case. Although the chromosome count of the normal male is 44 plus the sex chromosomes XY (often designated as 46, XY) and the chromosome count for the normal female is 44 plus the sex chromosomes XX (or 46, XX), a number of variations of these patterns appear. Individuals with Klinefelter's syndrome, for example, have an extra X chromosome, or 44 + XXY (47, XXY). Some people have two extra X chromosomes (48, XXXY). Are these people males or females? In both cases the individuals have two Xs, the assumed sexual configuration of a female, and they have one X and one Y, the assumed sexual configuration of a male. This is a crucial matter in certain contexts. For example, most international athletic competitions now require female athletes to undergo chromosome tests. These tests involve scraping a bit of mucus from the lining of the cheek. The mucus then is tested for the presence of Barr bodies. A Barr body, named after its discoverer, is the inactivated nucleus of one of two X sex chromosomes. This inactivation occurs only when at least two Xs are present. Hence, a Barr body is taken as evidence for femaleness. (The organizers of international competitions actually use the classifications of female —one or more Barr bodies—and nonfemale—no Barr bodies—to decide female eligibility, but for purposes of logical analysis, we consider bifurication into female and male.) The 47, XXY and 48, XXXY persons all have Barr bodies, as do normal females (46, XX) and individuals with extra Xs (47, XXX and 48, XXXX). If the Barr body test is the sole basis for a decision, the XXY and XXXY people must be considered female, and yet they are phenotypically male. Conversely, phenotypically female persons with Turner's syndrome, who lack one X sex chromosome (45, X), must be classified as not female because they lack the Barr body badge of femaleness. Obviously, neither the presence nor the absence of the Barr body invariably identifies genetic and functional sex, nor does the presence of a Y sex chromosome, because some genetic males are born with uteruses or other female genitalia, just as some genetic females are born with penis-like clitorises and scrotums (usually traceable to aberrations in the fetal development, Money & Ehrhardt, 1972).

Fetal aberrations are particularly likely to occur with male development. In the human case, it is often said that nature's basic plan is that of the female. Three changes must occur to produce male development. First, a mullerian-inhibiting substance prevents the normal development of the mullerian ducts into a uterus, fallopian tubes, and upper segment of a vagina. When this substance fails in a genetic male, a boy is born with a uterus and fallopian tubes in addition to normal male internal sex organs. Second, gonadal androgens must be produced to control many aspects of male differentiation, including male external genitalia and various organizational patterns in the brain. When fetal androgens are absent the male fetus will develop female reproductive anatomy. A third additive, related to the second, is that an enzyme, 5-alpha reductase, must be present to convert testosterone into its metabolite, dihydrotestosterone. Although most fetuses who lack this enzyme do not survive, those who live typically have ambiguous external genitalia and are often thought to be girls. Figure 2.2 shows examples. This condition is known as the androgen-insensitivity syndrome.

Female sexual differentiation also may be affected by excessively high intrauterine or fetal blood levels of androgens. In this situation, the androgenital syndrome, a girl is born with an enlarged clitoris, or, rarely, with a normal-looking penis and an empty scrotum (Money & Ehrhardt, 1972). An illustration appears in Figure 2.3. The presence of these aberrations in fetal sexual development and the variations in sex chromosomes give additional evidence that no single biological discriminator or other type of gender cue is likely to invariably and infallibly distinguish between females and males.

What can we learn from these cases of atypical sexual development? By following their psychological development as females or males, we can explore the interaction between the genetic blueprint and cultural-social-

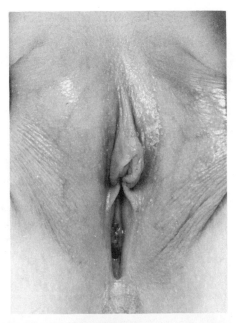

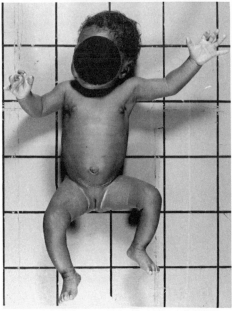

Figure 2.2   The top panel shows the female sexual appearance in a child with the androgen-insensitivity, testicular feminizing syndrome. The karotype is 46, XY and the gonads are testicular in histology though totally sterile. The bottom panel shows a newborn baby with the androgen-insensitivity, testicular feminizing syndrome, indistinguishable in appearance from a normal female. Reprinted by permission of the Johns Hopkins University Press and Dr. John Money from *Man and Woman, Boy and Girl*, by J. Money and A.A. Ehrhardt.

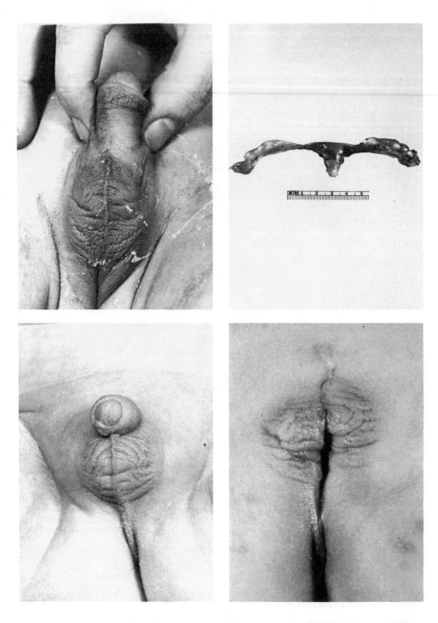

Figure 2.3   Two examples of phallic differentiation into a penis instead of a clitoris in genetic female (46, XX) babies born with the masculinizing adrenogenital syndrome. One was assigned and corrected as a girl (bottom) and the other as a boy (top). Reprinted by permission of the Johns Hopkins University Press and Dr. John Money from *Man and Woman, Boy and Girl* by J. Money and A.A. Ehrhardt.

psychological factors. Parents of these children decide to raise their children as males or females, so that the genetic heritage and the gender of rearing do not always match. These situations differ from the typical ones, in which genetic heritage coincides with the gender role of rearing. We might expect the biological and the sociopsychological factors to interact as shapers of our gender identity and gender behavior.

Some investigators have argued that genetic factors are more important determiners of gender-identity than cultural ones. Others, including Money and Ehrhardt (1972), disagree. They have reported that the way children are raised during their preschool years affects the gender role they assume and their gender identity. That is, if a genetic male is raised as a girl, he will act like a girl and will think of himself as a girl. This evidence suggests that cultural factors may override genetic ones. Money and Ehrhardt also describe females who had been exposed to excessive androgens during their prenatal development. These girls were considered by the investigators to be tomboys and to display more masculine behavior than a nonandrogenized control group. Presumably all of the girls had been raised as females. These latter results suggest the importance of biological factors when the social milieu and the genetic background are compatible, but they have been extensively challenged (e.g., Ehrhardt & Meyer-Bahlburg, 1981; Rogers & Walsh, 1982; Rubin, Reinisch, & Haskett, 1981). The investigators and the parents of the androgenized girls knew about their background and may have inadvertently expected them to behave in "masculine" ways.

A similar problem compromised the results of another report of predominant biological control. In this case, Imperato-McGinley, Peterson, Gautier, and Sturla (1979) monitored the gender roles assumed by males with a deficiency of the enzyme 5-alpha reductase. This syndrome is quite widespread in the area of the Dominican Republic where the study took place. Eighteen of these androgen-insensitive males (pseudohermaphrodites) reportedly had been raised as girls. During puberty, however, normal plasma testosterone levels produced more typical adult sexual and secondary sexual characteristics. Subsequently, 17 of the 18 subjects supposedly changed to a male-gender identity and 16 of the 18 adopted a male-gender role. At first glance, the results appear to support the authors' contention that the gender-role change was hormonally induced. Further investigation shows that the subjects, their parents, and others in their environment may have known about the syndrome and socialized the subjects accordingly. The authors even report that, "the affected children and adults in the Dominican Republic are sometimes objects of ridicule and are referred to as *quevedoce, quevote* (penis at 12 years of age) or *machihembra* (first woman, then man)." The results must be considered inconclusive.

Thus, the strongest evidence to date tilts toward the view that cultural factors have a marked effect on the development of gender roles and may even override biological messages on some occasions. This perspective in no way denies or diminishes the biological contribution to gender development, of course.

As psychologists, we were fascinated by the cultural-social-psychological aspects of gender development, especially with cues that serve as gender markers. In our culture, both sexes occasionally have short hair, just as both occasionally have long hair. Both often wear similar, "unisex" clothes, just as they often wear different kinds of clothes. Both may be affectionate, aggressive, independent, and warm depending on the situation. In brief, the cues that may be used to identify gender are numerous and elusive.

Tests of Gender Cues

One way to identify these cues is to test adults. Even though this information would not explain how the adults learned to identify and use the cues, it would anchor the quest for gender cues at the adult end. This kind of experimentation is obviously easier than trying to ascertain children's gender markers, since, as adults, we usually have some insight into the gender cues we use regularly, even though we may no longer recall the cues we used as children. We can use our own and others' introspection to define cues to be tested. Moreover, we can capitalize on adults' ability to provide a running verbal record of the reasons for their choices (as best they can ascertain and describe them). These abilities may be somewhat limited in the adult, but, by contrast, similar abilities of young children are scanty and typically unrefined. Thus, although for a comprehensive knowledge of the development of gender cues we will need to test children of various ages, we also need to assess the gender differentiators used by adults.

Adults' Gender Cues

What cues do adults use to identify gender? Even this question is elusive, because a relatively limited set of cues has been tested. Adults use genital cues more than body contours, and body contours more than hair length, according to Thompson and Bentler (1971). The investigators asked college students to dress anatomically correct, nude dolls. The genitals, body type (rounded breasts and hips for females; muscular, sinewy shapes for males), and hair length (long, short) were systematically combined, requiring a total of eight dolls. Each subject was asked to dress one doll, selecting the clothes from an assortment of female and male garments. In contrast to the adult results, four-, five-, and six-year-old children relied most heavily on hair length, then on body type, and least on genital cues when performing the same task. These results suggest that there are developmental changes in gender markers.

The Thompson-Bentler experiment is useful because it contrasts the performance of adults and children. It also describes a method of examining the relative importance of different kinds of cues, the matching of clothes with dolls that possess various physical characteristics. It does not, however, indicate whether these cues, all selected by the experimenters, are the ones that the subjects would use to distinguish gender if they were given a choice, nor does it assess the accuracy of the subjects' gender identification. In addition, the task seems considerably more appropriate for children than for adults. Indeed, one can't help but wonder what the adults thought about the task and the reasons for administering it to them. Did they respond seriously to the task or did they take it as a joke? We do not know.

Kessler and McKenna (1978) expanded the number of possible figures to 96 by using various combinations of overlays to create their stimulus figures. The cues were long or short hair, wide or narrow hips, breasts or a flat chest, body hair or no body hair, a penis or a vagina. In addition, the figures were unclothed, clothed in a unisex shirt and pants, or clothed in either the unisex shirt or the unisex pants. Five women and five men saw all 96 figures, answering the following questions for each figure: Is this a picture of a female or a male? Using a scale of 1 to 7, where 1 means not at all confident and 7 means very confident, how confident are you of your answer? How would you change the figure to make it into the *other* gender?

What were the results? Consider first the responses when the genitals were covered (when the figures were wearing pants, only). We might expect the two sexes to be named equally often because half of these figures had predominantly "female" characteristics and the other hand had predominantly "male" characteristics. Instead, 69% labeled the genital-covered figures as male. Kessler and McKenna interpret this result in terms of a predisposition toward the male in our culture. They support this interpretation by observations that the "female" cues were considered male by at least 55% of the subjects, whereas the "male" cues were treated as female by no more than 36%. When the genitals were uncovered, 96% of the figures with a penis were called male, regardless of the other characteristics. The vagina was not nearly as effective a single cue. Indeed, they found that even adding one more "female" cue to a vagina increased the proportion of times the figure was called female to only 81%. Adding two female cues to the vagina increased the proportion of times the figure was called female to about 95%. The most "female-like" combinations were, in addition to a vagina, wide hips, covered breasts, long hair and no body hair, breasts and long hair. Thus, a single male feature, a penis, produced slightly more labeling of the figure as male (96%) than *three* female features (95%). Moreover, as might be expected from the above, the viewers were most confident of their gender assignments when the figure had a penis. Kessler and McKenna conclude that, for adults, "gender attribution is, for the most part, genital attribution; and genital attribution is essentially penis attribution" (1978, p. 153).

Despite the large number of stimulus combinations tested, Kessler and McKenna's procedure tested a limited set of possible gender-differentiating cues with only 10 respondents. This is a very small sample. Moreover, it does not estimate how accurately the subjects can identify gender, because the "real" gender of the figures is indeterminate. Their procedure has certain advantages, however. It tests the effectiveness of sizable numbers of potentially gender-relevant cues, and it assesses the subject's confidence about the gender assignments. Presumably, the more easily and definitively the cues divide the stimulus persons into the two sexes, the more confident the subjects would be about their assignments.

Thus, although Kessler and McKenna's task does not identify the cues that subjects would select to identify gender, if they had an opportunity to do so, their results strongly suggest that, when assigning gender, adults will use (a) genital cues if those cues are visible, and (b) combinations of cues (such as hair length and body contours), if genital cues are obscured. In addition, when the stimulus figure has the same number of typically female and of typically male characteristics, the subjects are more likely to call the figure male than female, suggesting a male "bias."

Children's Gender Cues

Do children use the same cues? Apparently not. The typical finding is that young children use hair length and clothing to attribute gender, rather than genitalia or body contours (e.g., Brieland & Nelson, 1951; Conn, 1940; Katcher, 1955; Levin, Balistrieri, & Schukit, 1972; McConaghy, 1979; Thompson & Bentler, 1971). These results must be interpreted cautiously, however, because the only cues tested were those selected by adult experimenters. These cues may or may not be the ones the children would voluntarily select if they have a choice. The strongest conclusions that we can draw from this research are that, when faced with a limited set of cues, children rely on hair length and clothing, rather than genitalia, as gender differentiators; whereas adults show the opposite pattern.

Problems with Adult-Defined Cues

These results raise a number of questions. Perhaps the first is why have the investigations focused on this particular limited set of cues? One reason is that the adult investigators selected cues they thought they themselves used to assign gender. Genitalia may be considered the most reliable differentiator, unless the genitalia are not visible. For clothed persons, one must rely on less direct indicators, such as hair length, clothing, and body contours (secondary sexual characteristics). Another reason is that certain cues—

particularly genitalia—are deemed to be important by theories of gender development, as discussed in the next chapter.

Another question is why haven't the researchers studied subject-selected gender cues? This approach sounds desirable, but it is difficult to implement. Some method must be found that permits the children to identify for the investigator the cues they use to distinguish between the sexes. The work of Fagot (1985, Experiment 2) and Thompson (1975) has demonstrated compellingly that children are able to make these distinctions. Their ability to accurately label individuals as female or male is not in dispute. What is in dispute is the basis for their accurate gender attribution. The problem comes in trying to gain insight about the basis. When the subjects are young children, this difficult problem is hard to solve. Preschoolers are not always articulate, they are not always cooperative, and they are not necessarily able to label the cues or to understand the motivation for their choices. One possibility for solving this problem is to rely on mainly nonverbal methods of assessing relevant cues, such as asking children to draw a picture of each sex. This approach has its costs and benefits, too. The costs include the fact that the drawings of female and male figures may be difficult to interpret because the children's artistic abilities are not yet well developed. A related cost is that children may not have the ability to represent the cues they actually use for gender attribution. Despite its drawbacks, this technique imposes a minimum number of constraints on the children and offers the opportunity to identify cues. The relevance and salience of these cues can be further tested by presenting them to other children for gender attribution. That is, the procedure generates a set of drawings that can be analyzed for gender markers. The drawings can be shown to other children who are asked to say whether a girl or a boy is pictured. This is the procedure we used to initiate our search for the markers used by youngsters to attribute gender to others. The approach and the results are described in Chapter 4.

Gender Concepts: Gender Identity and the Gender Constancies

The salient gender differentiators for children may be related to the children's understanding of various gender concepts. These concepts include gender identity (awareness of one's own gender), temporal gender constancy or gender constancy or stability (recognition that gender typically remains the same throughout one's lifetime), and situational gender constancy or simply gender constancy (recognition that gender remains the same under various transformations such as wearing clothes or playing games usually associated with the other sex). A fourth type of gender constancy is occasionally identified—that called "motive" or the awareness that one's own gender cannot change even if one wants it to (Eaton & Von Bargen, 1981;

Wehren & De Lisi, 1983). Of course, this latter constancy could be modified by knowledge of pharmaceutical and surgical alteration of gender-related physical characteristics. Children with unstable gender identities might not be as sensitive to gender-related cues as children with stable gender identities. If so, children with unstable gender identities would make fewer correct gender attributions than children with stable gender identities.

Children learn to accurately label their own gender (gender identity) before they are aware that sex is virtually unchangeable over time or situations (e.g., Coker, 1984; Eaton & Von Bargen, 1981; Emmerich, Goldman, Kirsh, & Sharabany, 1977; Fagot, 1985; Marcus & Overton, 1978; Slaby & Frey, 1975; and Wehren & De Lisi, 1983). Knowledge of temporal gender constancy (stability) seems to appear next, followed by situational gender constancy. The situations over which gender remains constant vary considerably, of course. Wehren and De Lisi (1983) predicted that constancy over psychological traits (for example, associating gentleness and similar expressive traits with females and aggressiveness and similar instrumental traits with males) would be learned before gender constancy across activities and appearances because the visible or implied physical characteristics of the stimulus persons do not necessarily change across manifestations of different personality traits. That is, actual or implied physical changes are not likely to complicate the judgments. Moreover, changes in activities and especially in appearances are likely to involve stimulus transformations, so gender constancies in these areas should be acquired later than gender constancies for personality traits. Systematic age trends appeared with temporal gender constancy (stability) preceding gender constancy. The predicted age trends for gender constancies across personality traits, activities, and appearance did not emerge.

Wehren and De Lisi (1983) also analyzed the reasons children gave for assigning particular traits, activities, and so on to girls or to boys. Most of the three-year-olds gave no explanation for their correct gender constancy judgments. These children, who responded accurately to the questions about gender constancy but could not explain their answers in terms of constancy, are described as showing a "pseudoconstancy." A few others mentioned societal norms or "real" constancy of gender. Five-year-olds were somewhat more likely than the three-year-olds to use societal norms or real constancy. Seven- and nine-year-olds showed a continuation of these trends, with most nine-year-olds citing real gender constancy as the explanation for their correct gender constancy judgments. Incorrect gender judgments were typically given no explanation or a societal norm explanation. Apparently, the ability to articulate the understanding that a person's sex or gender remains constant across numerous transformations does not emerge much before age nine.

Pseudoconstant responses have been reported by a number of other investigators (Emmerich, Goldman, Kirsh, & Sharabany, 1977; Eaton & Von

Bargen, 1981). These responses may represent a transitional step in the attainment of real (true) gender constancy, as Emmerich et al. (1977) have proposed, or they may reflect nothing more than an inability of some three- and four-year-olds to articulate the rationale used by adults. An additional complication is that children are notoriously resistant to changing their classifications or statements once those responses have been made (e.g., Medin, 1973). If the first thing they say does not correspond to the scoring key for awareness of the particular gender concept, they may be unwilling to give another response, even though they might be able to do so. In fact, the children are rarely encouraged in these experiments to elaborate on their reasons. It is also possible that a kind of response output interference operates. In this situation, the respondent has a number of responses that could be made. Only one can be uttered or performed at any one time. While one response is being executed, others may be forgotten or become less accessible.

Regardless of the interpretation of pseudoconstancy, which must be held in abeyance at this time, the occasional mismatch between children's performance and their explanations raises questions about the relation between actions and the ability to articulate a rationale or logical basis for the actions. Not only do children show pseudoconstant responses in connection with questions about the gender constancies, they give seemingly unrelated, sometimes illogical, even nonsensical explanations for accurate gender attributions (Kessler & McKenna, 1978). Consequently, it is important to try to assess children's knowledge of these concepts with behavioral, largely nonverbal measures. The verbal measures, such as asking children to explain their responses are useful, too, as a way to try to make sense of the change from mismatch at early ages to match in the elementary school years.

The preceding studies support some conservative conclusions. Because systematic sex typing of activities and tasks requires the accurate association of the activities with gender, (a) gender identity and gender attribution develop concurrently, (b) these gender-related concepts precede the development of the concepts of temporal gender constancy (stability), (c) situational gender constancy develops still later and at about the same time across different kinds of situations, (d) the ability to verbally explain gender constancy and gender attributions is not always well-formed in the preschool, although (e) it is by age 9.

Contents of Gender Concepts

Our initial experiments, described in Chapters 4 through 6, focus on the cues used in gender attribution and on their changes with age, because of the central importance of this distinction in most societies. We then turn to the contents of children's gender roles, asking about the components of the concepts children have about femaleness and maleness and how these components of gender roles relate to gender attribution and the various gender constancies.

A brief introduction to the research into components of gender roles was presented in Chapter 1 and this introduction will be complemented, as appropriate, in Chapters 6 through 9. In this chapter, to complete the review of general literature related to gender concepts, I go into somewhat greater detail, occasionally mentioning both advantages and disadvantages of particular methodologies.

What components might be associated with gender concepts? The possibilities seem staggering, but some areas are particularly salient candidates. As Huston (1985) tells us, the two sexes are thought to perform different activities, have different interests, manifest different personality characteristics, demonstrate different kinds of behavior in social situations, use language in different ways, and so forth. For our purposes, the issue of whether or not the two sexes actually exhibit these differences is less important than what people, particularly children, attribute to the two sexes, and this latter is our focus. Let us consider the evidence for two broad classes. The first consists of activities and interests, and the second encompasses personality and social attributes.

Activities and Interests

What are the beliefs about the activities and interests of the two sexes? Sometime after their second birthdays, children begin to demonstrate gender-typed toy preferences. That is, when given a choice, they are more likely to select a toy stereotypically associated with their own sex or to assign toys in a stereotypic way to a male or female stimulus person (Blakemore et al., 1979; Falkender, 1980; Fein, et al., 1975; Liss, 1981; O'Brien, Huston, & Risley, 1983; Pitcher & Schultz, 1983; Schau et al., 1980).

Similarly, by the time they are three years old, children have developed distinct, gender-stereotyped preferences for their play activities (Fagot, 1974, 1978; Kuhn et al., 1978; Smith & Daglish, 1977; Thompson, 1975). They also recognize gender differences in the activities typically pursued by others, including adults (Edelbrock & Sugawara, 1978; Flerx et al., 1976; Huston, 1983; Marantz & Mansfield, 1977; Masters & Wilkinson, 1976; Schau et al., 1980).

Preschoolers also have a wealth of information about gender differences in occupations. Gettys and Cann (1981) found that even at the ripe age of two and one-half years, 78% of their respondents pointed to a male doll when asked to indicate which doll (male or female) had the job of construction worker. In contrast, 23% pointed to the male doll for the job of teacher.

When asked what they want to be when they grow up, four- and five-year-olds provide pronouncedly stereotyped responses (Garrett, Ein, &

Tremaine, 1977; Huston, 1983; Kleinke & Nicholson, 1979; Marantz & Mansfield, 1977; Nemerowicz, 1979; Papalia & Tennent, 1975; Thornburg & Weeks, 1975; Tremaine & Schau, 1979). Young children do not necessarily have accurate information about adult occupational roles, however, as shown by two quotations from Beuf (1974). In this case, the children were asked what they would do if they were the other sex. A boy answered, "A girl? Oh, if I were a girl I'd have to grow up to be nothing" (p. 143). Perhaps equally distressing was a girl's response, "When I grow up I want to fly like a bird. But I'll never do it because I'm not a boy" (p. 143).

What happens to these occupational views as the children mature? Various investigations of elementary school children suggest that stereotyping becomes increasing rigid up to about the fourth grade and then begins to decline (Cann & Haight, 1983; Cummings & Taebel, 1980; Gettys & Cann, 1981; O'Keefe & Hyde, 1983; Tremaine, Schau, & Busch, 1982). The decrease in stereotyping of occupations in grades five and six may occur because the older youngsters are learning more about the many opportunities that are available to both sexes.

These results impressively document the rather amazing ability of even preschoolers to detect, store, and be able to act on gender-related differences in activities and interests.

Personality and Social Attributes

Despite their awareness of stereotyped activities of adults as well as children, preschoolers seem to have little information about personality traits often associated by adults with one or the other sex (Etaugh & Riley, 1979; Flerx et al., 1976; Kuhn et al., 1978), although Reis and Wright (1982) noted that some traits, such as "cries a lot" were assigned reliably more often to a female figure than to a male one whereas "cruel" was assigned more often to the male than to the female figure. These investigators found increasing stereotyping of personality attributes with age.

This increase in the stereotypic assignment of personality characteristics has been documented by others, as well (Best et al., 1977; Davis, Williams, & Best, 1982; Williams et al., 1975), but the increase slows as the children reach the fifth and sixth grades (Meyer, 1980). The pattern of development thus seems to be similar for activities and interests and for personality characteristics: Preschoolers gradually acquire the gender-stereotypic views of their culture and this process continues through about the fourth grade. They then seem to become aware that, although the two sexes may differ in general, substantial overlap occurs in real life.

There are some troublesome aspects of the personality research that argue for reserving judgment about the evidence. Most of the work has used a paradigm proposed by Williams, Best, and their colleagues (e.g., Williams

& Best, 1982). In this paradigm the children have to assign each personality trait to either a woman or to a man. They are not allowed to say that both sexes might show the trait, nor are they able to indicate the relative strength of the trait for each sex. Hence, these estimates of children's gender-typing of personality traits may have been distorted by the demands of the task. This possibility motivated the experiments reported in Chapter 7.

Finally, we, like most other researchers, embraced the obvious assumption that the contents of children's gender concepts will vary. Some girls are likely to include many traditionally feminine traits and relatively few masculine ones; others will show the opposite. Boys, too, presumably will show quite a range of gender concept components. This rather pedestrian assumption becomes interesting when we ask about the consequences, such as whether or not these concepts relate to adjustment, as some theorists claim? We sought an answer in the experiment presented in Chapter 8.

Summing Up

We began this chapter on sex, gender, and their interaction by noting that no single differentiator exists that can be used to infallibly assign sexual organisms to two classes, female and male. The sex of the organism is not invariably determined by the genetic heritage it receives at the time of conception nor do organisms' sex always remain unchanged during their lifetimes (even excluding pharmaceutical and surgical interventions). For example, for some turtles, the temperature of incubation of the fertilized ova determines sex; for some fish, a female may convert to a male following the loss of a male from the school, and the reverse also occurs. This information from lower animals should make us skeptical of simple correspondences between genetically determined sex and the gender identity and gender roles assumed by individuals.

Indeed, this is the case, as demonstrated by Money and Ehrhardt (1972). They have found that the gender of early rearing, rather than sex, has a pronounced influence on the gender the child assumes, in addition to the gender-related roles the child espouses. Despite this intriguing evidence that environmental and cultural factors may affect development, even occasionally overriding genetic inheritance, in most cases, such as those we consider in our research, genetic sex and the gender of rearing coincide.

How do human beings identify the sex of other humans? The answer to this question is quite simple when we are talking about adults. They use genital (actual or implied) cues, cues based on secondary sexual characteristics, and, to a lesser extent, cues based on clothing and hair length. The answer is much harder when we are talking about children. We can say that children rarely use cues based on genitalia and secondary sexual characteristics. There is some evidence that they use hair cues, probably hair length, although investigators have not always specified how the hair was varied. They may also use clothing.

The ideal way to ascertain the cues children use is to have them inform us. But how? Children are notoriously inarticulate about the bases for their actions. Their skills as artists may not be well enough developed to capture and convey cues that are really critical. Nonetheless, the use of their drawings, amplified by their explanations, seemed to be the most promising way to begin such investigations, and this is the procedure used in Chapter 4.

The ability to identify the sex of others (or what is usually called "gender attribution") may be related to other information children have about gender, such as what sex they are themselves (gender identity), their knowledge that their sex remains the same over time (temporal gender constancy), their knowledge that they cannot change their sex even if they wanted to (motivational constancy), and their knowledge that their sex remains the same even when they engage in activities often associated with the other sex (situational gender constancy). Although, children do seem to acquire gender identity before the gender constancies, this knowledge is not yet clearly linked with other information about gender roles. We pursue these issues in Chapters 4 through 8.

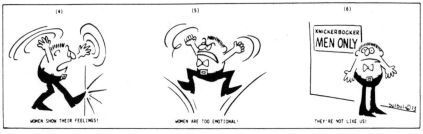

Cartoon from *I'm not for women's Lib.*

CHAPTER 3

Theories of Gender Attribution, Gender Roles, and Their Development

The castration complex of girls is also started by the sight of the genitals of the other sex. They at once notice the difference and, it must be admitted, its significance too. They feel seriously wronged, often declare that they want to "have something like it too," and fall a victim to "envy for the penis," which will leave ineradicable traces on their development and the formation of their character and which will not be surmounted in even the most favourable cases without a severe expenditure of psychical energy. (Freud, 1933).

The girl's nature as biologically conditioned gives her the desire to receive, to take into herself; she feels or knows that her genital is too small for her father's penis and this makes her react to her own genital wishes with direct anxiety; she dreads that if her wishes were fulfilled, she herself or her genital would be destroyed...The boy, on the other hand, feels or instinctively judges that his penis is much too small for his mother's genital and reacts with the dread of his own inadequacy, of being rejected and derided. Thus his anxiety is located in quite a different quarter from the girl's, his original dread of women is not castration anxiety at all, but a reaction to the menace to his self-respect. (Horney, 1967)

Historically, theories of gender development and relevant research have been intertwined; they formed a "feedback" loop. Assumptions from the theories have stimulated research, and research results have sparked theoretical insights and modifications. In this chapter, we consider theories that have been applied directly to the development of concepts of gender. The selection of the principal models was easy. These models explicitly address the development or acquisition of gender concepts by human beings. Other, more tangential models, such as cerebral lateralization, were included largely

29

because of the current interest in this topic, whereas theories whose human applications represent mainly generalizations from other levels of the phylogenetic scale, such as sociobiology, were excluded. We leave it to history to judge the seriousness of our omissions.

In our coverage of theories of gender we examine assumptions about gender identity, gender constancy, and gender roles. The theories' hypotheses about how these gender concepts originate, develop, and contribute to gender roles yield important predictions. These hypotheses already have influenced the selection of gender cues for experimental testing, and they have been used to predict the changes that should occur with maturation, as well as other variables that should interact with gender attribution. We begin with psychoanalytic, cerebral lateralization, social learning, cognitive developmental, and cultural-genital theories, and end with gender schema and cultural schema models. Last, we list some of the major, testable predictions from the various theories and models that will be examined in the rest of the book.

Psychoanalytic Theory

Best known is Freud's psychoanalytic theory. He assumed that the anatomical differences of males and females produce different kinds of mental (psychological) reactions and different experiences. Herein lies the basis of his famous (infamous?) contention that "anatomy is destiny." On Freud's view, young children learn that they either do or do not have a penis. Learning that one has a penis is, according to Freud, tantamount to learning that one is a boy. Learning that one does not have a penis is tantamount to learning that one is a girl. As Kessler and McKenna cogently remark, "Freud saw gender identity as so intrinsically tied to genitals that he did not even consider it necessary to provide the theoretical underpinnings of that connection. Nor does he explain how children learn to see genitals as the dichotomizing feature by which they distinguish all people and categorize themselves" (1978, pp. 85–86).

In general, Freud assumed that human personality develops as a series of psychosexual stages. Presumably, the child passes through the stages of early childhood, the oral, the anal, and the phallic, during the first six years. Because these stages form the basis for subsequent stages, they are the most critical. Gender differentiation appears during the phallic stage.

During this stage, somewhere between the ages of three and five, children develop largely unconscious wishes to possess the other-sex parent and to eliminate their closest rival, the same-sex parent. This complex is resolved by identification with the same-sex parent and a renunciation of the other-sex parent. For example, boys think and fantasize about their mothers, their primary caregiver and "love object." This fixation is called the Oedipal complex (after the Greek myth about Oedipus, who killed his father and married his mother). They quickly learn, however, that their father has a prior claim on the mother, a claim that conflicts with their desires. Thus, the father becomes a threatening rival. This conflict induces a fear, which also may be fantasized, that the father will castrate them (the castration complex). This fear is resolved by allying themselves with their father. Boys express this process by copying their father's behavior, mannerisms, dress, and so forth. It is through this identification with his father that the son acquires the qualities of maleness possessed by the father and develops his own gender identity. The male gender identity is further characterized by a mature conscience or superego, an exalted personality development that Freud minimized in women. The conscience or superego is formed as the child internalizes the negative sanctions of society, the "shalt-nots." Young males also must relinquish their alliance with their mothers by extending the father-imitation process to seeking affiliations with women other than their mothers.

The process by which girls come to identify with their mothers is less clear in Freudian theory. An early catastrophic event for young girls is their realization that they do not have a penis; they have been "mutilated" by having the penis removed; they are deficient. Young girls are attracted to males, the complete persons who possess the magical penis, particularly their fathers. Thus, girls become attached to and fantasize about their fathers (the Electra complex), much as young boys become attached to their mothers. Further, the girls then are in competition with the mother for the father's affections. The next step is obscure, for Freud posits that girls think they have already been castrated. There should be no fear of castration that binds them to their mothers as they learn that all females lack a penis. They develop feelings of contempt for other females and blame their mothers, who share this inadequacy, for their own deficiency. Nevertheless, girls somehow come to identify with their mothers, they begin to imitate and to model their own lives after their mothers. In the final stage of normal female development, the young woman becomes interested in men as an avenue to having a surrogate penis, the carrying of a child.

As a consequence of the psychosexual stages, Freud attributed the traits of passivity, masochism, and narcissism to the female personality. Presumably, the passivity develops while the girl is waiting for the father to impregnate her. Impregnation also requires masochism (penetration) and may result in the subsequent pain of childbirth. Narcissism and jealousy are hypothesized to be involved in all of the above. In addition to these rather negative traits, Freud denies women the development of a mature superego (conscience). He tells us that the superego of girls

is never so inexorable, so impersonal, so independent of its emotional origins as we require it to be in men. . . That they show less sense of justice than men, that they are less ready to submit to the great necessities of life, that they are more often influenced in their judgments by feelings of affection or hostility— all these would be amply accounted for by the modification in the formation of their superego which we have already inferred. (Freud, 1948, pp. 196–197)

The above quotation is a translation and, as such, may not capture all of the nuances of Freud's approach. Nevertheless, the quotation and the preceding account illustrate two prominent aspects of psychoanalytic theory. First, its emphasis on the biological substrate of gender development implies that virtually all boys should follow one stage-defined sequence and girls should follow another. Deviations reflect delayed or arrested progress through the appropriate stages. The second aspect is that female personality, derived from inadequate biology, is destined to be less mature than male personality.

The foregoing describes only those aspects of the theories devised by Freud and his followers (psychoanalytic theory) that are particularly relevant to our purposes; psychoanalytic theory is far more complex and comprehensive than the above description suggests.

In general, psychoanalytic theory predicts that children first learn about their own genitalia and then acquire information about gender roles. All gender differentiation originates with a recognition that one does or does not possess a penis, a view that is contradicted by research. For example, two specialists in psychosexual development, Money and Ehrhardt (1972) note that some children with penis-like genitalia have female gender identities, whereas others without penises have male gender identities. The key to gender identity seems to be the gender of rearing, not the external genitalia. That is, children who are raised as girls, think of themselves as girls and call themselves girls, even when their genitalia look like penises, and boys, raised raised as boys, consider themselves boys, again regardless of the appearance of their genitalia. As discussed in Chapter 2, the apparent shift of androgen-insensitive males (pseudo-hermaphrodites) from a female gender identity to a male identity with the advent of testosterone-enhancing puberty (Imperato-McGinley, et al., 1979) does not seriously challenge this conclusion. Moreover, children can accurately attribute gender to pictures of strangers whose genitalia are covered (e.g., Coker, 1984; Thompson, 1975). In addition, Freud's equation of gender identity with genital awareness is challenged by the evidence that children rarely use genitals as gender differentiators, even when the genitals are shown (McConaghy, 1979; Thompson & Bentler, 1971). Thus, a *literal* view of penis envy is not supported. Numerous studies, however, have documented greater widespread valuing of the male role over the female role, a view that might be considered a *symbolic* form of penis envy, as Kessler and McKenna (1978) contend.

But that is not the only problem for the concept of penis envy. Males may envy female sexual and reproductive capabilities. In example, Mead

(1963) describes the "couvade" ritual among the Arapesh. During childbirth the father moans and groans, screams, and carries on to a much greater extent than the mother. According to one anecdote, an anthropologist commented that a middle aged man was in good physical condition. "Yes," came the response, "but you should have seen him before he had so many children." During pregnancy, too, the father may experience typical symptoms of pregnancy. Variations of "womb-envy" are occasionally reported, in the United States and in other countries.

Obviously, Freud's theory does not accommodate these results. A possible counter is that the developmental process may go awry: On occasion, children may fail to progress through one or more stages and thus would show disturbed or arrested gender development. This position founders on three points. First, children do not equate genitals with maleness and femaleness, although they reliably distinguish between the two sexes. It is hard to believe that faulty gender development would be sufficiently widespread to explain these results in terms of abnormal gender development. Second, psychological gender identity does not invariably correspond to genetic sex; and third, children do not rely on genitalia to identify gender (or sex) of others.

Not only do the data fail to support predictions of psychoanalytic models, but these models are vulnerable on other grounds, as well. Most important is Freud's belief that the unconscious is a driving force of human behavior. The unconscious simply is not available to contemporary experimental procedures. This is a case, then, of formulating untestable postulates. The same charge has been made about many of Freud's concepts, such as penis envy and the Oedipal complex.

Still other problems plague Freud's theories. The ideas that led to his theories were derived from his work with patients. These individuals, all of whom presumably considered themselves sufficiently troubled to seek medical assistance, were not necessarily representative of others. Additionally, as noted above, Freud's dependence on anatomy (biology) to drive the system does not allow for the multiple influences of culture, society, and learning. Despite these conceptual empirical difficulties, Freud's psychoanalytic ideas and those of his disciples continue to influence contemporary perspectives of gender development, particularly among nonpsychologists, and it is important to evaluate their merits as explanations of contemporary research on gender concepts.

Some Variants of the Psychoanalytic Theme

Most of the descendant theories agree that genital awareness leads to fantasies about the opposite-sex parent, which leads to identification with the same-sex parent. The child's gender role develops as a consequence of this identification. Two particularly interesting psychoanalytic theories merit further discussion for our purposes, because both try to explain more fully how females, as well as males, acquire gender identity. The first was proposed by Horney quite some time ago (1926); the second was introduced by Chodorow 50 years later (1976).

Horney (1926) postulated that girls focus not on the absence of a penis but on the presence of a vagina. The vagina elicits anxiety because it is internal, not easily inspected, and probably too small for the fantasized (large) penis of the father. Girls may show some penis envy, because they assume that people with penises are able to masturbate easily, but this envy is replaced by an appreciation of the vagina in the birth process, as long as normal gender development occurs. Horney also notes that some penis envy may reflect a recognition of the greater societal power of people with penises, the males (a symbolic penis envy). Males fear that their penises will be too small for the fantasized larger genital of their mothers and that they will be subject to ridicule, scorn, and derision. Thus, boys fear the loss of their self-respect. Although Horney's views seem more contemporary than those of Freud, they adopt a genital-based gender role development and are, therefore, subject to the same disconfirming research that contradicts Freud's approach.

Also particularly relevant to gender attribution and to gender role development is Chodorow's (1976) view that emphasizes the role of maternal parenting. Most children are cared for by one or more women; hence, both girls and boys develop early attachment to these maternal figures. At later ages, they seek to return to this emotional state. This is relatively easy for men to achieve within a heterosexual relationship, even though they simultaneously fear exclusive domination by women. Women have more difficulty. They typically are expected to enter into adult heterosexual relationships, but these relationships are likely to be secondary to the primary attachment they feel toward maternal figures. To resolve this paradox, women are more likely than men to cultivate close ties with members of their own sex, in addition to those with the other sex. The result is that women, more than men, are able to minister to the emotional needs of both sexes. Chodorow's view suggests, then, that young children of both sexes will share many traits typically considered feminine. As they mature, females will continue to demonstrate these traits, whereas males will diverge in a masculine direction. This view also implies greater male than female dissatisfaction with their gender roles, an implication that diametrically opposes a Freudian prediction but which is relevant to our experiment on adjustment and gender roles.

What does the evidence say about these predictions? Are young children more like their mothers than their fathers? Do boys come to resemble their fathers while girls continue to take after their mothers? In general, the answers are negative (e.g., reviews by Biller, 1976; Lamb, 1976; Maccoby & Jacklin, 1974). Boys' traits do not show the predicted shift from feminine to masculine; feminine mothers do not seem to have particularly feminine daughters any more than masculine fathers have particularly masculine sons. As Lamb notes (1976, page 13), "the only consistent correlate of paternal masculinity is the femininity of daughters" (Heilbrun, 1965; Johnson, 1963; Mussen & Rutherford, 1963; Sears, Rau, & Alpert, 1965).

To sample two more psychoanalysts, we briefly consider the views of Deutsch and Erikson. Deutsch (1944) extended Freud's psychosexual stages for women from puberty through adulthood. Supposedly, it is during adjustment to adulthood that women's sexual satisfaction shifts from the male-related "aggressive" clitoris to the "mature" vagina. Through this shift the woman achieves the goal of a passive personality. It is this personality that enables her to await impregnation and her true role as a mother. In many respects, Deutsch espoused many of Freud's ideas. Another disciple, Erikson (1964), differed by emphasizing gender identity as being constantly subject to change throughout the lifespan of the individual. Moreover, he construed women as having not an envy of the penis but a sense of their own creative "inner space."

There are common themes running through most of the psychoanalytic perspectives. Hence, they tend to be vulnerable to the same kinds of criticisms. These themes may be summarized as follows. The development of gender identity, gender constancy, and gender roles depends initially on the child's recognition of the genital differences between the sexes. The child fantasizes about the other sex parent as a love object, but, through various anxiety-driven mechanisms, comes to fear the other-sex parent and to identify with the same-sex parent. As part of this identification, the child imitates the same-sex parent, and thus typically acquires gender-typed characteristics. At a later maturational stage, the child must again come to value the other sex as a love object. These views suggest that genital cues should be the most important and effective gender markers at all ages. Indeed, if children are not aware of *genital* differences, they should not be aware of *gender* differences. These theories suffer from the numerous conceptual weaknesses and from contradictory experimental evidence, as already noted.

We have gone into some detail about psychoanalytic approaches because they have been and continue to be astonishingly influential, in spite of conceptual weakness and contradictory evidence. It is the case that Freud and his followers deserve credit for making the topic of sex one of both public and scientific interest. They deserve credit for devising theories of gender development which stimulated research in this area. Nonetheless, from a historical perspective, psychoanalytic theories of gender development no longer seem very fruitful.

Cerebral Lateralization

From many perspectives, this view is not a "theory." It might appropriately be termed a model, although the early formulations, in particular, were primarily restatements of the data (see Sergent, 1983).

Before describing this approach, I digress briefly to explain why I am not treating general sex-related differences of brain structures (sexually dimorphic brains) in detail. One reason is that this area of research is in a state of flux, with new and sometimes contradictory findings occurring so rapidly that it is difficult to evaluate them. It seems prudent to wait to apply this area of research to the understanding of human gender concepts until it has yielded a body of definitive, well-accepted, and cohesive results. Another reason is that most of the work has been done with lower animals, and a direct extension to humans is tenuous. A third reason is that the role of experience is just now being incorporated into the animal research. Finally, some peripheral structures may supplement or mediate sexual dimorphic responses, but the role of these structures is not yet clear. For reviews of this research as it applies to human beings, see Bleier (1987), Kimball (1981), and Moore (1985).

The cerebral hemispheres are intriguingly asymmetrical. The obvious question is why? What purpose could nature have had in producing such structures? We know that, in most people, and certainly in most right-handers, major language centers are located in the left hemisphere. These findings led to the hypothesis that the left hemisphere might be specialized for processing language and linguistic-type, sequential materials. Subsequent work showed somewhat greater right hemisphere domination in certain visuospatial tasks. It seemed, at least for a short time, as though the two hemispheres have somewhat different tasks. The left deals with linguistically-relevant material, whereas the right deals with visuospatial materials. As we shall see, this view was almost immediately assaulted by research findings that complicated the picture.

Before continuing, I should explain how this research is conducted. To be valid, this kind of research must be conducted with great care. Until fairly recently, the technology was not equal to the demands of testing visual input, although it was adequate for carefully conducted tests of auditory material.

In general, the research plan is to present a task to one and only one hemisphere. This is difficult in the normal human being, because the corpus callosum, a network of fibers that connects the hemispheres, serves as a relay station. One way of obviating this problem is to capitalize on the basic structure of the system. The functional plan of the body is to have the left side represented in the right (contralateral) side of the brain and vice versa. This means that to test the relative efficiency of the left hemisphere for processing a language task, the experimenter would compare performance (perhaps the speed with which words are recognized) when the words were presented to the right ear (left hemisphere connections) and when the words were presented to the left ear (right hemisphere connections). Similarly, to test visual recognition of words, the words must be delivered to the right *half* of an eye (for left hemisphere connections) or to the left *half* of an eye (for right hemisphere connections). This kind of work takes sophisticated equipment to be sure that only the intended portion of the eye is stimulated. Many experimenters have tried to achieve this goal by presenting the stimulus to one side of the center for such a brief interval that eye movements presumably are precluded. A more recent, and more satisfactory technique is to use a computer that senses eye movements and moves the briefly displayed stimulus with the eye. For completeness, I should mention that there are connections made with the brain on the same (ipsilateral) side of the body, as well, but these connections tend to be suppressed.

Let us return to the left hemisphere-language, right hemisphere-spatial activities view. This view was met by some puzzling results. For example, melodies seemed to be processed more efficiently by the right hemisphere for musically unsophisticated persons, whereas the melodies seemed to be processed more efficiently by the left hemisphere for musically trained individuals (Segalowitz, Bebout, & Lederman, 1979). How can we account for these findings? One possibility is to expand the earlier model to include not only the mode (type) of material but also the kind of processing. The commonality between musicians' processing of melodies and the general processing of language may be the kind of detailed, sequential, analytical processing that is required. In contrast, the nonmusicians' processing of melodies may be based on treatment of the melody as a unit, a sort of global entity, which resembles the processing of a picture or other visuospatial input. Hence, a modified approach was constructed. It claimed that the functional asymmetries may be considered evidence of a hemispheric specialization, in which each hemisphere has its own mode of information processing and cognitive style (Gazzaniga & LeDoux, 1978).

How would such a view explain differences between the sexes, including concepts of gender? Again, the story requires a slight detour.

About this time, Maccoby and Jacklin (1974) and others published reviews suggesting that females tend to obtain somewhat higher scores than males on tests of verbal ability, whereas the opposite occurs for mathematical and spatial ability and for aggression. Buffery and Gray (1972) proposed that the left hemisphere becomes dominant for language functions earlier in girls than in boys and that early specialization for language function reduces bilateral processing of spatial information. As a consequence, females show greater left hemisphere lateralization; boys show greater right hemisphere lateralization. Some research supported the latter but not the former view

(Newcombe, 1982; Sherman, 1978). Adding complexity to the situation, some specific spatial tasks for which males often excel do not seem to be associated with the right hemisphere (Kimball, 1981; Waber, 1979).

Various modifications were introduced in an attempt to accommodate the data (see Levy, 1972; Sherman, 1978, for a review). One fairly recent one (Harshman & Remington, 1976, cited in Sherman, 1978) is that lateralization increases with age. Because girls mature faster than boys, they do not develop as much lateralization, so that, as adults, they show less lateralization. Early in development, however, they show somewhat more than males, who have not developed to the same extent. Another possibility is that hemispheric specialization may be related to gender differences in the corpus callosum, with a posterior portion (the splenium) being larger and more bulbous in women than in men (de Lacoste-Utamsing & Holloway, 1982). Presumably, the size of the splenium is related in some as yet undetected way to the degree of hemispheric symmetry.

There are a number of problems with these views, in addition to those already mentioned. As with psychoanalytic models, one major difficulty is the diversity of abilities evinced by the two sexes. The performance of the two sexes on both verbal-linguistic and visuospatial materials overlaps to such an extent that the sex of the performer accounts for only 1 to 4% of the variance (Hyde, 1981). These observations contradict the predictions of substantial uniformity of performance among females and among males which must be made by the lateralization and psychoanalytic models.

The models also fail to readily accommodate the effects of the environment. If gender differences in these abilities were innate, and, perhaps, immutable, we would expect them to withstand cultural and learning experiences. This assumption has been falsified by a number of reports. I cite two, which should suffice to illustrate the point. First, in countries where reading is considered a "male domain," boys read as well as girls (Johnson, 1973-74). Second, three hours of training on spatial tasks was enough to eliminate differences between female students and their male colleagues on four tests of spatial ability (Stericker & LeVesconte, 1982).

Even if there were robust gender differences in verbal and spatial ability to explain, the evidence amassed to date does not support the inferences that have been made. For example, as Bleier (1987) comments, there are no data linking hemispheric specialization (lateralization) with improved visuospatial ability. At our current state of knowledge, it is just as probable that greater bilateral recruitment is more beneficial than greater specialization. In fact, more extensive bilaterality presumably would offer greater protection than unilateral representation against permanent damage from cerebral accidents, such as those produced by strokes and head injuries.

Even the evidence of differential specialization as a function of either age or corpus callosal development is based on severely limited numbers of observations and unsupported inferences, as pointed out by Bleier (1987) and by Bleier, Houston, and Byne (1986). An early report of differential aging of the hemispheres (Geschwind & Behan, 1982) is a case in point. These investigators reported that left-handedness, some disorders of the immune system, and some developmental learning disabilities (e.g., dyslexia and stuttering) were more commonly associated in boys than in girls. They hypothesized that left handedness implicates right hemispheric dominance, although other evidence suggests that 70% of left-handers show the standard configuration of language dominance in the left hemisphere (Rasmussen & Milner, 1977). Geschwind and Behan further proposed that prenatally secreted testosterone slows the development of the left hemisphere. The result is right hemispheric dominance in males. Unfortunately, although they cite another investigation which studied a large number of fetal brains (507, to be exact), they did not acknowledge the *absence* of sex differences in the more extensive research (Chi, Dooling, & Gilles, 1977). Other criticisms could be advanced (see Bleier, 1987), as well, but the message is clear. We must conclude, on the basis of the findings collected to date, that sex differences in the structure of the hemispheres have not been demonstrated.

A similar conclusion emerges from an examination of the evidence about sex differences in the splenial portion of the corpus callosum. The initial work by de Lacoste-Utamsing and Holloway (1982) was based on a sample of 14 brains (5 female and 9 male). They did not provide information about the age of the patients, the cause of death, or the method of selection of the brains, all potentially relevant factors, so each of these variables could have affected the condition of the brains. Bleier and her associates (Bleier et al., 1986) were unable to replicate the central finding that splenial width was greater for females than for males. Once again, the data do not provide much support for the notion of cerebral sex differences that might underlie gender concepts or other types of gender differentiation.

Still another challenge to these models comes from the increasing evidence that, under all normal conditions, both hemispheres of intact individuals are recruited to at least some extent (Sergent, 1983). Consequently, this approach does not predict gender differences in, say, spatial and linguistic ability.

It seemed advisable to consider this cluster of models in substantial detail because, although the current state of knowledge is not very encouraging, some people remain convinced that sex-differentiating cortical structures drive gender-related cognitive functions.

Social Learning Theory

In contrast to psychoanalytic theory's emphasis on internal processes, such as fantasies, envies, castration complexes, and Oedipal-Electra complexes, social learning theory stresses the learning or imitation of behaviors that are considered consistent or inconsistent with a particular gender role. Behaviors considered consistent or appropriate are rewarded, whereas behaviors that are taken as inconsistent or inappropriate are punished. This reinforcement may take many forms, such as smiles, money, praise, punishment, attention, and scoldings. We depend upon other people for the recognitions signaled by the rewards in our environment. Recognition, itself, indicates attention from others. Hence, recognition may be personally valued, even if it involves punishment, scolding, or other forms of seemingly negative attention.

Social learning theory (Kagan, 1964; Mischel, 1966, 1970), assumes that gender-typed behaviors are acquired and maintained through the same processes that are used to acquire and maintain other kinds of behaviors. These processes, in addition to positive and negative reinforcement, include observational learning, generalization, and discrimination. Children come to learn, through differential reinforcement, what is approved or disapproved by others (e.g., parents, teachers, and peers) in their environment. They may initially engage in a behavior because they have seen another do it (Bandura & Walters, 1963). This, of course, is observational learning (imitation). A good example is a television commercial showing a boy putting on aftershave lotion as he imitates an older male who is getting ready for a date. Imitation is not restricted to live models, for it is possible for children to imitate "symbolic" models whom they have read about or have seen on television or on film.

For observational and differentially reinforced learning to be useful, children need to be able to extend (generalize) behavior to similar appropriate situations. In addition, to be able to behave in such a way that they are rewarded and not punished, they need to be able to identify the behaviors with certain situations that are or are not associated with specific rewards— that is, they must learn to discriminate. These same processes, differential reinforcement, imitation, generalization, and discrimination also shape other kinds of learning.

As children learn about behaviors considered appropriate or inappropriate for their sex, they come to value those behaviors perceived as appropriate and to devalue those that they assume are inappropriate. In addition, children learn to attach labels to the two behavior constellations and to themselves ("girl," "boy"). As Kohlberg (1966, p. 89) explained, with reference to social learning, a little boy thinks, "I want rewards, I am rewarded for doing boy things. Therefore, I want to be a boy." Thus, social learning theory assumes that knowledge about gender roles either precedes or is acquired at the same time as gender identity, in contrast to the order prescribed by a psychoanalytic perspective.

How does social learning theory fare in the harsh scrutiny of research evaluation? Quite well, to the extent that children are aware of gender-typed activities, toys, and occupations at about the same time they are able to identify their own gender (Thompson, 1975). Less well, to the extent that parents do not always seem to reward their girls and boys in different ways for their gender-typed behavior. In their survey of relevant articles, Maccoby and Jacklin (1974) did not find that parents treat their sons and daughters differently, for the most part. Others disagree, however (e.g., Block, 1978). Indeed, recent research has shown differential reinforcement of girls' and boys' behavior by not only parents (e.g., Armentrout & Burger, 1972; Burger, Lamp, & Rogers, 1975; Langlois & Downs, 1980; Snow, Jacklin, & Maccoby, 1983; Tuddenham, Brooks, & Milkovich, 1974) and teachers (Cherry, 1975; Levitin & Chananie, 1972; Serbin, O'Leary, Kent, & Tonick, 1973), but by peers, as well (Langlois & Downs, 1980). Gradually, substantial support for the differential reinforcement hypothesis has accumulated.

Social learning theory continues to fare less well to the extent that children learn about the constancies of gender after they learn gender identity (e.g., Coker, 1984; Marcus & Overton, 1978; Slaby & Frey, 1975). Nevertheless, the gender-identity-before-gender-constancy order does not seriously compromise social learning theory, for this theory addresses basic gender concepts, not their refinements, extensions, or advancements. More troublesome is the evidence that people hold somewhat different views of their own gender traits and those of either the typical member of their sex (Spence, Helmreich, & Stapp, 1975; Lohaus & Trautner, in press; but see Davis, Williams, & Best, 1982) or of most members of the same sex (our laboratory), and the passive nature of the assumed process. From an early age, children monitor their own behavior, saying, "Boys don't cry," "Boys don't play dolls," "Girls don't get dirty," "Girls can't play hockey," and the like. These statements reflect the children's concepts about the gender roles associated with the two sexes, concepts that are not a part of social learning theory.

Observational learning or imitation encounters problems as well. If it is to predict why girls tend to develop "girl-like" behavior and boys tend to develop "boy-like" behavior, it must predict that children are more likely to imitate same-sex than other-sex models. Maccoby and Jacklin (1974) assessed this possibility by reviewing 23 studies. They reported no consistent tendency for youngsters to imitate same-sex models. Similar results were reported in a more recent review of more than 80 studies (Barkley, Ullman, Otto, & Brecht, 1977). If children are as likely to copy their fathers or other male models as to copy their mothers or other female models, there is no principled basis for explaining the acquisition of gender-stereotyped behavior.

At least a partial reprieve has been provided for social learning theory by Perry and Bussey's (1979) version. They propose that children observe the different frequencies with which members of each sex perform tasks in specific situations. The youngster uses these frequencies to form abstractions of female- and male-appropriate behavior in given situations. It is as though, through observation, the child samples behavior in certain settings, noting what each sex does. After having obtained these samples, the child forms representations of the kind of behavior that is appropriate (consonant with the child's sex) to imitate in the situations. Such "computational" models are increasing in popularity in many areas of psychology, in part because they assign an active and interactive role to the observer. The most effective way to provide an introduction to this model is to quote Perry and Bussey (1979):

> It is our contention that the typical investigation designed to explore same-sex imitation has employed an experimental paradigm that is conceptually remote from how imitation actually contributes to sex role development and therefore that the null results of much of the previous research on same-sex imitation constitute an inappropriate base for rejecting the same-sex imitation hypothesis. In the typical investigation, children are exposed to a single (often familiar) male and/or female performing (often novel) responses and are then tested for imitation of the models' responses... In the real course of development, children discern what behaviors are appropriate by watching the behavior of *many* male and female models and by noticing differences between the sexes in the frequency with which certain behaviors are performed in certain situations. They then use these abstractions of sex-appropriate behavior as "models" for their own imitative performance. (p. 1700)

Overall, earlier forms of social learning theory seem incomplete as models of gender-concept development. They focus on objective behavior, on what can be observed. Such an approach creates problems for predicting both the similarities and the differences in gender roles. To explain similarities, this theory must rely on cultural uniformities, on substantially homogeneous but different experiences by girls and by boys. It therefore must predict that the gender roles considered appropriate for self will be similar or identical to those held for most members of the same sex. Social learning theory does not deal with either the underlying cognitive mechanisms or with possible biological and/or maturational influences, except as these factors modify reinforcement contingencies. Finally, it treats children as passive entities being shaped and honed by the forces in their environment. Of course, children operate on their environments in the senses of selecting behaviors from their behavioral repertoires, of imitating others, of generalizing and discriminating between situations, but they do not play active roles in interacting with and structuring their environments. This active role is an essential component in Perry and Bussey's (1979) promising modification of social learning theory, and it is at the heart of the next theory, the cognitive developmental model.

Cognitive-Developmental Theory

According to cognitive-developmental theory, gender roles develop as an interaction between a person's heredity and environment, as naturally as other maturational processes do, such as walking and talking. We develop different gender attitudes because we have had different interactions in the past. Such a perspective could explain commonly observed cross-cultural sex differences, including the social pre-eminence of the male. The major proponent of this view, Kohlberg (1966), likens the process to Piaget's notions about cognitive development. Piaget believed that cognitive development evolves through distinct conceptual stages. Each stage evinces specific thought and reasoning processes. For example, preschoolers often think that there is more water in a tall thin glass than in a squatty fat glass, even though they had watched an experimenter pour the water from one glass to the other. The children's reasoning process differs from that of their elders, not because it is "wrong" or "misguided," in the traditional sense, but because it represents an earlier stage of cognitive development. As Kohlberg (1966, p. 82) tells us, "This patterning of sex-role attitudes is essentially 'cognitive' in that it is rooted in the child's concepts of physical things—the bodies of himself and others—concepts which he relates in turn to a social order that makes functional use of sex categories in quite culturally universal ways. It is not the child's biological instincts, but rather his cognitive organization of social-role concepts around universal physical dimensions, which accounts for the existence of universals in sex-role attitudes."

Piaget contends that, as children mature, their cognitive organizations undergo radical transformations. At an early age, usually until about three-and-a-half to four years of age, children learn the identities of objects, including themselves. These objects, however, are not seen as invariant. Instead, the objects may change from place to place or condition to condition, as the example with the water illustrates. Kohlberg's application to gender development posits that at this stage children know their own gender identities, just as they know their names, but they are not yet aware of gender constancy. They form what Kohlberg calls a "cognitively stable" sexual identity during this critical period and this identity is markedly resistent to change. By the time children become aware that physical objects have non-varying identities, they also become aware that their gender identities are invariant. Kohlberg assumes further that the self-categorizations determine values, so that children who label themselves as boys also value boy-related objects, activities, occupations, and other things. Girls show the same general patterns. This assumption, like that of psychoanalytic theory, assigns priority to gender identity. Children first learn to label their own sex, then they seek roles related to their sex.

When children have become aware of the constancies, they value and seek experiences assumed to be related to their gender identity. This process is fostered by differential reinforcement from significant others and by imitation. Children are particularly likely to attend to authority figures. Because they have a tendency to associate authority with size (adults, who are large, have authority over children, who are small), children also may value males over females. Thus, once children have the scaffolding of gender identity and the gender constancies, they then build upon it all of the trappings of gender roles.

Variations in gender roles occur because children have different experiences, some of which may even produce distortions in the cognitive organization of the female or the male role. These distortions explain individual differences in gender roles, including such relatively uncommon gender patterns as transsexualism.

Briefly, then, cognitive-developmental theory holds that "feminine" (or "masculine") behavior results from the acquisition of a female (male) gender identity. By contrast, social learning theory posits that a female (male) gender identity results from rewards for same-sex behavior, punishments for other-sex behavior and imitations of same-sex models. A central prediction of cognitive-developmental theory is that children should develop a gender identity before they acquire gender constancy and other information about gender roles. The gender-identity-as-a-prerequisite view has been difficult to test, because by the time that children have the language skills to answer the question of whether they are a girl or a boy, they also correctly answer questions about paper dolls, and tend to show gender-typed toy preferences (O'Keefe & Hyde, 1983; Thompson, 1975). The coexistence of these abilities means that it is impossible to know which came first. This problem may be solved by novel research paradigms at some time in the future.

Other evidence is supportive. For example, some researchers have found that gender identity precedes the development of the gender constancies (Emmerich et al., 1977; Marcus & Overton, 1978; Slaby & Frey, 1975).

Nevertheless, cognitive-developmental theory has been criticized on a number of counts. One is that the ability to correctly answer the question, "Are you a little girl or a little boy?" does not necessarily imply the existence of a concept of gender identity or even an awareness that gender is a property of people. Children are told repeatedly that they are little girls or little boys, and their ability to correctly answer the gender identity question may not disclose anything about their understanding of abstract gender concepts. They may be repeating, almost parrotlike, the labels they have heard applied to themselves—just as they can state their name or the color of their hair or their eyes. This criticism is one that could be leveled at all of the theories, of course. A second, more damaging criticism is that children should become sensitized to gender cues in the order of themselves, others of the same sex, and others of the opposite sex. Although children typically learn about gender cues relating to themselves, such as gender identity, before they learn about cues relating to others, they do not always acquire gender information about others of the same sex before others of the opposite sex (e.g., Fagot, 1985; Wehren & De Lisi, 1983; but see Eaton & Von Bargen, 1981). Instead, gender cues related to self are acquired before gender cues related to others regardless of the sex of the others (Eaton & Von Bargen, 1981; Fagot, 1985; Gouze & Nadelman, 1980; Marcus & Overton, 1978; Wehren & De Lisi, 1983). Third, the theory relies on the concepts of reinforcement and imitation to explain variations in gender role behavior. This last criticism is not particularly serious, for there is no strong reason why these processes should not also affect the developmental process.

Cultural Genital Theory

Kessler and McKenna (1978) advance a different perspective. They abandon the commonly held notion that gender concepts are associated with physical genitalia, in part because children correctly attribute gender without using either genitalia or secondary sex characteristics. Instead, they propose that people construct "cultural genitals" to refer to gender. "Cultural genitals" consist of either having or not having a "cultural" penis, the trappings of maleness associated with male advantage, preference, and influence. This latter assumption is partially derived from their findings (described in Chapter 2) that when a figure had a penis, it was usually labeled as male, regardless of the number of female-like characteristics it had. Figures lacking a penis were usually called females. They propose that we assign cultural genitals regardless of whether or not individuals are clothed. Moreover, these cultural genitals are such potent constructs that they can override physical genitalia when a discrepancy exists. To illustrate this point, Kessler and McKenna describe the experiences of a male-to-female transsexual who had not had genital surgery. Her (male) lovers "did not treat the (physical) penis between her legs as a (social) penis. They seemed to have decided that it was 'all right' that Janet *appeared* to have an inappropriate physical genital because they had already decided that the genital had no reality in a cultural sense" (Kessler & McKenna, 1978, p. 154; all parentheses and italics are from the original).

On the Kessler-McKenna model, cultural genitalia and their associated gender-role attributions are reflexive and circular, in the sense that each affirms the other. Thus, having a cultural penis affirms tendencies to behave in male-like ways, and behaving in male-like ways supports the inference of a cultural penis. Further, the child's socialization process links with the cultural genital associations of gender role behaviors, dress, linguistic conventions, and the myriad ways that occasionally mark gender. The result is the development of a schema, a cognitive structure that can be used to categorize. No single cue is sufficient to identify a male from a female, but combinations of cues are used. When deciding about gender, the principle that is used is, "See someone as female only when you cannot see them as male." (Kessler & McKenna, 1978, p. 158). Thus, a critical prediction of this model is the pre-eminence of male cues for gender attribution.

The cultural genital model is so new that it has not been tested except by one experiment conducted by Kessler and McKenna with 10 adult subjects. This experiment does not really address our questions about the origins of gender concepts because, in addition to the very small number of participants, the use of adults does not illuminate early instigating and formative features of gender-concept development. The gender concepts of adults have been evolving for such a relatively long time that the origins and processes contributing to gender concepts are exceedingly difficult to capture. The other experiment described in their book was with children, but the design was not directly relevant to the notion of a cultural genital.

Gender Schema Models

Recent newcomers to gender models are the gender schema views. These views share the proposition that people develop a schema for gender. That is, individuals construct a cognitive structure or schema of the traits, behaviors, activities, attitudes, and the like that are associated with a particular gender. This schema serves as an organizer of perception and behavior. We may perceive events that are consistent with our schemata, just as we may fail to observe events that are inconsistent with our schemata. Both the cognitive-developmental and the cultural-genital theories also entail schemata, but schema development is not as central to them as it is to the gender schema models.

The rub with respect to gender schemata comes with the assessments of these schemata. What are their components? Do the components typically correspond to personality traits stereotypically assigned to women and to men?

Answers to these queries have evolved as related research has matured. Early approaches presented lists of stereotypically "feminine" and "masculine" personality traits to people, who were asked to identify the traits they possessed or to indicate how much of each trait characterized their own selves. These techniques yielded estimates of the self-endorsements of traits commonly associated with the two sexes. Researchers often classified respondents into one of four groups. People who claimed that they had many "feminine" but few "masculine" traits were called "feminine," regardless of their biological sex. Similarly, those who claimed many "masculine" but few "feminine" traits are considered to be "masculine." Still others endorsed both "feminine" and "masculine" traits to a substantial degree and were called androgynous, whereas those who endorsed relatively few of either "feminine" or "masculine" traits were considered "undifferentiated," to use the terminology introduced by Spence, Helmreich, and Stapp (1975). According to this version of gender models, one's gender concepts reflected the balance of stereotypically "feminine" and "masculine" personality traits incorporated into one's belief system. Thus, both women and men can be "feminine" or "masculine," just as both can be "androgynous" or "undifferentiated." Early work (e.g., Bem, 1975, 1981; Spence et al., 1975; Spence & Helmreich, 1978) postulated further that the possession of substantial traits of both sexes (being androgynous) conferred flexibility of action which should be more effective and healthy than the possession of lesser numbers of these traits. Occasionally terms such as "expressiveness" and "instrumentality" are used instead of "feminine" and "masculine."

These views have been modified recently. Bem (1981, 1982) now contends that sex-typed people (feminine women and masculine men) are gender-schematic, whereas others are gender-aschematic. Because her revised model also contends that the personal gender schema is derived from (assimilated into) an individual's cultural knowledge about gender differences, only sex-typed people should exhibit clear gender schemata. Moreover, their cultural and personal gender schemata should be very similar. By contrast, Markus and her associates (Crane & Markus, 1982; Markus, Crane, Bernstein, & Siladi, 1982) posit that the only individuals who will be gender-aschematic are the undifferentiated. Masculine schematics will be particularly sensitive to characteristics associated with masculinity, but not to those associated with femininity, whereas feminine schematics will show the opposite effect, regardless of the sex of the person (i.e., both men and women with feminine schemata will be attuned to female-typed information, but not to male-typed items). Androgynous schematics will be sensitive to characteristics associated with both sexes.

Both theoretical and empirical problems plague these models. Theoretically, the assumption of two independent, orthogonal continua of "masculininity" and "femininity" (more accurately described as "instrumentality" and "expressiveness," respectively) is central to the basic philosophy of androgyny espoused by the models and to the underlying contention that individuals may possess personality traits from both constellations. This assumption unfortunately contradicts the other—unidimensional and bipolar —construct of gender schematization. The problem, then, is to reconcile the two constructs. Consider the definitional problem: If one is gender schematic, one must possess the diverse information about gender that constitutes a schema. Does this information necessarily include that for both sexes—is it simultaneously highly instrumental and highly expressive as we might expect for a gender schematic individual? Bem says no, that the highly gender-schematic person is a masculine male or a feminine female—in other words, a person with extensive same-sex gender information but possibly devoid of extensive other-sex gender information. By extension, the gender aschematic individual must be defined as one who has extensive gender information about the other sex, about both sexes, or about neither sex—a seemingly incongruous and heterogeneous group. Markus characterizes the gender schematic individual as one with extensive information about either or both sexes; the gender aschematic person lacks this information about both genders. In effect, then, this view logically amalgamates the twin assumptions of bidimensional expressive and instrumental continua with a unidimensional gender schema continuum by equating gender schematization with a disjunctive combination of instrumental and expressive continua.

Both Bem and Markus report results that generally, but not invariably, support their views. Other evidence is contradictory: Jones, Chernovetz, and Hansson (1978) found that men classified as gender-typed on the BSRI were *less* likely than others to use gender-related terms in self descriptions. Women did not show differences as a function of gender typing. In addition, self schemata are not always highly correlated with gender schemata assigned to typical females and males (Lohaus & Trautner, in press; Spence, Helmreich, & Stapp, 1975) or to most females and males (Intons-Peterson, in press). These results challenge both models, and they led Spence and Helmreich (1981) to conclude that gender-related personality traits as measured by the standard instruments assessing instrumentality and expressiveness are, at most weakly associated with sex role orientation, gender identity, and gender schema.

The above gender schema theories emerged from the adult literature on gender schemata; hence, they are noncommital about age changes in the contents of gender schemata.

Martin and Halverson's (1981) self-socialization gender model, however, arises from child research. They predict that the child's "own-sex" or "in-group" schema will develop before the "other-sex" or "out-group" schema. Furthermore, this model predicts that accurate gender identification precedes the development of gender schemata, because children must be able to identify the gender of people if they are to correctly classify gender-related information. Gender constancy, however, may be acquired simultaneously with gender schemata. Again, the evidence is only partially supportive. As already noted, children are able to identify toys and preferences for the other sex as readily as they identify them for their own sex (e.g., Nadelman, 1974; Thompson, 1975).

All of the gender schema models contend that individuals interact with their environments, actively constructing mental structures to represent their awareness of the events around them.

Cultural Gender Model

Next, we present our cultural gender model. Although schemata are important, our treatment emphasizes a separation between self or personal concepts and cultural gender ones. The former refer to concepts about one's self that include both gender-related and gender-unrelated information and the latter refer to concepts about information typically associated with the two sexes in one's culture. We assume that developmental changes occur in the contents and use of both kinds of concepts.

Our approach was described briefly in Chapter 1; we go into more detail at this point. We hypothesize that, from a very early age, children perceive gender-related information associated with each sex and that they incorporate this information into gender concepts. These gender concepts are cultural in the sense that they reflect what the child observes as "gender universals" at that particular time in development. Simultaneously, or slightly earlier, children begin to develop their personal or self concepts. These concepts include self-related items, such as name, eye color, hair color, and perhaps gender-related information. Gender information contained in the self concept does not necessarily duplicate the contents of the children's cultural gender concepts. For example, a little girl may think that most females are weak and unathletic but that she is strong and athletic, two characteristics that might or might not be included in her concept for most males. Both the cultural gender concepts and the self-concept will incorporate an awareness of gender constancy by about age seven or so.

In our view, the differences between members of a culture with respect to gender concepts will reside primarily in their self concepts. Thus, we consider people to be gender-schematic if their self-concepts contain many of the components from their cultural gender concepts. Further, we propose that, with age, individuals come to use a single principle to differentiate the gender of others—that of judging others against their cultural male concept. In other words, they formulate what we could call a "male protocol" or a "male pattern." If another person fits well with this protocol, the person is considered male and is treated like a male, regardless of what is or is not known about the individual's genitals or sex chromosomes. This operating principle emerges as an efficient way to distinguish between the two sexes, an activity that is strongly encouraged—indeed, demanded by our society.

Predictions of The Theories

This review allows us to identify the gender cues that each of the theories assumes is important to gender concepts and to gender attribution. These predictions offer a basis for comparison of the theories and for evaluating their predictive success. The theories also make a number of other predictions, often difficult to test experimentally. We postpone discussion of these less tangible predictions until Chapter 9.

1. Freudian psychoanalytic theory. Physical genitalia are the earliest and most salient gender markers for all ages.

2. Variants of psychoanalytic theories. Variants that stress the role of the mother in the child's early development must predict that female-related cues are more salient gender markers at early ages than male-related ones. This asymmetry should disappear with age.

3. Cerebral lateralization. The different versions of older cerebral lateralization models presumably would predict that males should perform better than females on mathematical and spatial tasks, whereas females should perform better than males on verbal tasks. Although we did not test our participants on tasks specifically chosen to be verbal or spatial, many of the tasks required explanations of their choices and were, therefore, verbal in nature. More recent models, which assume the recruitment of both hemispheres, would not predict gender differences because our tasks were reasonably complex.

4. Social learning theory. Girls and boys should show different reinforcement histories with respect to gender-related behaviors. Further, according to the Perry and Bussey (1979) formulation, they should imitate gender-appropriate behavior of same-sex models more than either the gender-inappropriate behavior of same-sex models or than gender appropriate behavior of other-sex models.

5. Cognitive-developmental theory. The development of gender attribution and gender schemata depends upon, and therefore follows, the development of both gender identity and gender constancy. Moreover, size should be a gender marker.

6. Cultural genital theory. Male-related cues should be preeminent at all ages.

7. Gender schema models. Bem (1981, 1982) suggests that gender-schematic persons (feminine women and masculine men) will hold gender-specific schemata for both sexes, whereas gender aschematic individuals will not. Markus (Crane & Markus, 1982; Markus et al., 1982) proposes that feminine- and masculine-schematics will hold schemata for femininity, or for masculinity, as the case may be, but not for the other gender. Only androgynous schematics will have gender schemata for both genders. Martin and Halverson (1981) predict that gender schemata for one's own gender will be stronger than schemata for the other gender.

8. Cultural gender model. This view expects young children to develop gender schemata for each sex (cultural gender concepts), and self-concepts which may include components from either, one, or neither of the cultural gender concepts. Children formulate a gender-marker principle based on the presence (or absence) of male components.

We turn now to the cues children use to identify gender.

Boy drawn by a kindergarten boy

Girl drawn by the same kindergarten boy

CHAPTER 4

Gender Cues in Children's Drawings

As we have seen, children and adults do not necessarily use the same cues to attribute gender to others. When asked to identify gender, preschool children appear to use hair length and clothing, rather than genital cues or secondary sexual characteristics (e.g., Conn, 1940; Katcher, 1955; Levin, Balistrieri, & Schukit, 1972; Thompson, 1975; Thompson & Bentler, 1971). Adults rely mainly on genital or secondary sexual characteristics (Kessler & McKenna, 1978; Thompson & Bentler, 1971). Should we conclude from these results that gender markers change developmentally? Not yet, because most of these experiments have tested fairly restricted sets of cues. Some important cues may have been overlooked or even confounded with other cues. For example, Katcher (1955) refers to hair "style," although it seems that he actually varied hair length. More commmonly, "hair style" is used to refer to curly or straight hair, to bushy or head-hugging hair, and so on. In addition to hair length and hair style, hair comes in different colors. The hair styles and colors of the stimulus dolls and pictures are not described in the cited papers, so we cannot be sure that only hair length was varied. "Inconsequential," you say. But are these other hair cues inconsequential? Are they irrelevant? Only experimental testing will answer the question, but some casual observations suggested that children might use just such unreliable cues. As one blond curly-headed little boy told me, "I always know girls, 'cuz they have yellow curly hair. No, that's not right; sometimes, they have pigtails."

The moral of this tale is clear: We have no way of knowing what children use as gender cues until we give them a chance to tell us. Our a priori perceptions of hair or other cues as not sensible, unreliable, or even misleading should not deter us from giving youngsters the opportunity to demonstrate how they identify girls and boys. These considerations argue for the use of child-referenced materials. Such materials should minimize the bias produced by having adults select the cues, and they should facilitate the identification of gender cues relevant to children at various ages.

One way to approach this problem is to let children show us the cues they use to assign gender. To do this, we had preschool, kindergarten, and third-grade children draw pictures of a boy or man and a girl or woman. We assumed that "Drawings can be regarded as constructions in which parts are selected and combined in accordance with specifiable rules. This type of approach...links the study of drawing to other studies of representation and cognition...," as Goodnow (1978, p. 637) cogently noted. The logic then called for showing these pictures as stimulus materials in the next phase of the experiment: We asked other children in the same age groups to say whether the drawing showed a girl or a boy. With this procedure, adapted from one used by Kessler and McKenna (1978), we were able to identify gender cues used to *produce* the drawings, a method for teasing out Goodnow's "specifiable rules." Similarly, we could identify the cues used to *recognize* the two genders. These two sets of cues, one representing production and the other recognition, then could be compared. Note that we assume that the drawings are constructions, not "simply printouts" of perceptions (Olson, 1970, p. 19).

These advantages of child-referenced materials must be weighed against disadvantages of the technique. For instance, some cues may still elude adult detection. We may not always be able to unambiguously identify cues in the drawings, for the drawings are seriously constrained by the children's artistic abilities. "Imprecisely" or "poorly" drawn cues may be undecipherable even to age mates who might be able to respond to more accurately drawn pictures. The drawings may be unreliable. That is, children may draw the same "subject" in different ways at different times even though the instructions remain the same. This problem does not appear to be serious, because children tend to retain similar central-body characteristics in repeated drawings of human figures, although they may vary appendant parts such as arms and legs (reported in Goodnow, 1978). Then too, the children's verbal statements may not help. Kessler and McKenna's (1978, Chapter 4) amusing anecdotes indicate that these descriptions often are nondifferentiating (e.g., claims that girls have ears and boys have round eyes when the child draws ears and round eyes for both sexes), tautological (e.g., "It's a man because it is.") or nonexistent (e.g., "I don't know."), although Wehren and De Lisi (1983) successfully classified stated reasons into three groups: no explanations, explanations based on social norms, and explanations based on a true understanding of gender constancy. These explanations which seem illogical to adults clearly have a different ring for preschoolers, who frequently assume an air of patient condescension when an adult asks them to explain how they can distinguish between a girl and a boy when both have the avowedly critical ears and round eyes. I have had youngsters say to me, after a long, expressive, almost plaintive sigh, "This is a boy, because he has *round* eyes. This is a girl, because she has *round* eyes. *That's* how I know." The message being conveyed is that, as an adult, I'm not very perceptive and can't be expected to understand the obvious.

These problems can be at least partly circumvented by modifying Kessler and McKenna's design and by using an assortment of recognition and production measures. For example, we compiled an extensive sample of drawings by combining the drawings made by Kessler and McKenna's subjects with those generated by our participants. By increasing the number of drawings, the procedure also increased the pool of potentially gender-differentiating cues. The drawings were analyzed for gender-distinctive cues. These cues then were treated as "predictor" variables in the gender attribution tests to ascertain whether other children would systematically assign consistent gender labels. In short, we looked for converging patterns among the production and recognition measures.

It is possible that the particular gender differentiators the children prefer will depend on their stage of gender concept development. Children who are aware of temporal and situational gender constancy may choose different cues than children who are not yet aware of these constancies (Coker, 1984; Fagot, 1985; Kuhn et al., 1978; Marcus & Overton, 1978; Slaby & Frey, 1975). Accordingly, our design included tests of gender identity and of the gender constancies.

The gender attribution performance by children with various levels of gender constancies must be compared with the reasons they give for their choices. As discussed in Chapter 2, children may obtain correct scores on both the gender constancy and the gender attribution measures and yet not be able to explain their reasons. This type of circumstance, or pseudoconstancy, seems to be particularly characteristic of children below the age of four. In addition, Kessler and McKenna (1978) described the nonsequiturs, tautologies, and similar problems that challenged interpretation of the verbalizations preschoolers gave to explain their choices.

Were these problems due to insufficient rapport with the children, to insufficient probing of children's answers, or to preschoolers' infelicity with vocabulary and language? These questions are by no means trivial. While it is true that preschoolers are notoriously uncommunicative with strangers and have not yet developed the vocabulary of older people, accumulating evidence constantly reminds us of the amazing capacities of the very young. These capacities were obscured in the past by designs that were either somewhat insensitive or insufficiently attuned to children's capabilities and understanding. These considerations impelled us to ask our subjects to explain their answers in every case. Thus, we asked about the reasons for answers to the gender constancy questions and why each picture was called a girl (woman) or a boy (man), in addition to explanations of their responses to questions about the gender constancies.

To summarize, our first experiment focused on the following issues: Do children reliably assign gender labels to child-produced drawings? If so, what cues are related to the gender labels? Do these cues differ from those suggested by results with adult-selected materials? Is gender labeling related to gender identity, to two measures of gender constancy, gender invariance over time and gender invariance over situations, and to knowledge that they could not change gender even if they wanted to do so (what has been called "motive" by Eaton & Von Bargen, 1981, and Wehren & De Lisi, 1983)? Finally, do the children's verbalizations yield evidence of true gender constancy and of an awareness of the bases they use to assign gender labels?

The Procedures

We tested 60 lower-middle and upper-middle class children: 20 preschoolers (ages three and four), 20 kindergartners (ages five and six), and 20 third graders (ages eight and nine). Half of the children at each grade level were female and half were male. Approximately 10% of each age group were black and two preschoolers were Hispanic.

All of the children participated in two sessions. The gender attribution tests were presented during the first half of both sessions. During the second half of Session 1 each child drew one picture of a girl (woman) and one of a boy (man). During the second half of Session 2, each child was asked a series of questions about gender identity and gender constancy. The gender attribution tests were used as recognition measures of gender differentiators and the drawings, as production measures.

The materials used for the first gender attribution test were copies of the drawings generated by Kessler and McKenna's (1978) sample of preschool, kindergarten, and third-grade children in New York. Twelve drawings were assigned to each subject, four from each grade level, and these four contained two drawings that supposedly depicted males and two that supposedly depicted females. Each child's 12 drawings were presented in a predetermined, random order. The pool of New York drawings contained 20 pictures at each grade level. Each drawing was used equally often in assigning pictures to the sets of twelve to be shown to individual children.

Session 2's gender attribution test used the drawings that the children themselves had produced during the second half of Session 1. Each child saw 14 drawings: the child's own two drawings, and four drawings from each grade level that had been generated during Session 1. Each of these conditions contained equal numbers of "girl" and "boy" drawings. As with Session 1, the 14 drawings assigned to a given subject were shown in a predetermined, randomized order and each of the Session 1-produced drawings was assigned equally often over the group of subjects.

The test for gender identity and gender constancy (adapted from Coker, 1984, and Slaby & Frey, 1975) contained the following questions:

1. Are you a girl or a boy?
2. Are you a (opposite sex of child's first response)?
3. When you were a little baby, were you a little girl or a little boy?
4. Were you ever a little (opposite sex of child's first response)?
5. When you grow up, will you be a man or a woman?
6. Could you ever be a (opposite sex of child's first response)?
7. If *you* wore (opposite sex of child) clothes, (*child's name*) would you be a boy or a girl?
8. If *you* wore (opposite sex of child) clothes, would you be (an opposite sex of child's first response)?
9. If *you*, (*child's name*), played (opposite sex of child) games, would you be a boy or girl?
10. If *you* played (opposite sex of child) games, would you be a boy or a girl?
11. Could you be a (opposite sex of child) if you wanted to be?

We scored gender identity from Questions 1 and 2, temporal gender constancy from Questions 3–5, "motive" from Questions 6 and 11, and situational gender constancy from Questions 7–10.

All children were tested at their schools. For the two gender attribution tests, the experimenter explained that the child's task was to say whether the drawings showed a girl (woman) or a boy (man). The order of naming the sexes in the questions was balanced. After the child made a choice (statements of "don't know" or "can't tell" were accepted), the experimenter asked how she or he knew it was a ____ . This procedure was followed for all drawings of each attribution test.

In Session 1, the child then was asked to draw a girl or woman and a boy or man. Then the experimenter asked what made each drawing a girl (boy). In Session 2, the gender identity and constancy questions followed the gender attribution test. Session 2 followed Session 1 by one to two months.

Attributing Gender to the Drawings

Our initial concern is whether children accurately recognize the gender intended by other youthful artists. As Figure 4.1 suggests, our subjects, regardless of grade level, accurately labeled the gender of drawings produced by kindergartners and third graders, but not the drawings made by preschoolers.

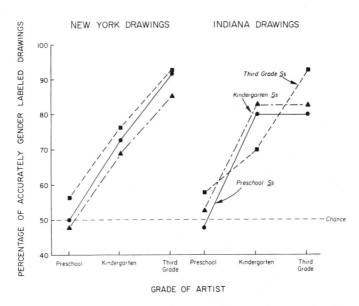

Figure 4.1   Percentage of accurately gender labeled drawings for the three school grades of artists in New York and in Indiana.

In general, then, the mean numbers of correctly labeled drawings tended to increase with the grade of the artists, F's$(2, 96)$[1] $= 44.72$ and 13.83 for the New York and Indiana drawings, respectively. The levels of responding were tested against chance-level performance for each grade of subject, grade of artist, and source of the drawings (New York, Indiana). Pictures drawn by kindergartners and third graders are accurately gender-labeled above the chance level (.05 or beyond) by all grades of subjects; pictures drawn by preschoolers are labeled at a chance level by all grades.

The analyses of variance cited above were conducted on the numbers of correctly gender-labeled drawings, with the subject's sex, grade, and gender sophistication (see below) as between-subject variables and the artist's grade as a within-subject variable. Separate analyses were performed for the New York and Indiana drawings. A similar analysis was performed on the children's own drawings, except that no within-subject variable existed (the artist's grade was identical to the subject's grade). The results of this analysis paralleled the two described above. All probability values are equal to or less than .05 unless otherwise stated.

---

[1] The results of standard statistical tests are included for readers who are interested in them. In general, results that are likely to occur no more than five times out of one hundred replications by chance alone (customarily expressed as $p < .05$) are considered to be statistically significant.

Both girls and boys showed the same patterns for each age group. This is an interesting result, because it suggests that our children were no more sensitive to gender cues from their own sex than they were to other-sex cues (also see Fagot, 1983; Wehren & De Lisi, 1983). Apparently, these children hold concepts for both sexes. These data, then, do not support Chodorow's (1976) contention that having primarily female caregivers sensitizes children to female-related cues (almost all teachers were women), nor do they suggest that children are differentially sensitized to male-related cues.

Cues Used to Designate and to Identify Gender (Production and Recognition Cues)

The next step was to identify the cues that were used to produce drawings of "females" and "males." We began by comparing the drawings with the descriptions given by the children. Would their explanations of why one of their drawings depicted a boy (man) and the other a girl (woman) make sense to adults? For the preschoolers, the answer is "Not much," but for the third graders, the answer is "Some of the time."

The preschoolers' explanations were delightfully inventive, although not very descriptive. These youngsters often explained that a circle which contained marks described as eyes, nose, and a mouth and with a few crayoned scratchings on top, was a boy because it had short hair; another circle with the same set of facial features and similar scratchings on top was a girl because it had long hair. Figure 4.2 illustrates this case. There was a variant on this theme: Sometimes both of the drawings were hairless (see Figure 4.3). One little boy announced that he had drawn his daddy: "See, this is my daddy. I know he is my daddy because he has a hole in his shoe." Indeed, inside the circle that was a foot was a black dot. His drawings of his mommy also had a black dot inside the circle-foot, although he said that his mommy had earrings on (the earrings were not decipherable). Another child announced that her drawings showed a boy and a girl "because I make 'em." Still others refused to explain. All together, most of the "explanations" appealed to various characteristics of the hair.

The kindergartners used hair characteristics just as often as the preschoolers. The major difference was that the characteristics they named as showing that the drawings depicted a boy or a girl were apparent in the drawings. The kindergartners' strong tendencies to accentuate hair differences are shown by Figures 4.4–4.6. A few of them gave unexpected explanations, such as "Boys have black and red hands and feet and girls have blue hands and feet," and "This is a boy so I have to make him pink. This is a girl so I have to make this one purple."

The third graders cited hair in almost every case—and many of them even mentioned the three prominent hair variables of length, color, and style. For example, one boy anticipated the overall results when he explained that the girl had long, yellow, curly hair and the boy had short, brown, straight hair! These children drew much more elaborate figures, adding fingers, clothing details, and sometimes objects in the background. Overall, however, the reliance on hair variables as gender differentiators fairly leapt out at us.

Charming and occasionally amusing as the children's comments were, we needed to describe the contents of the productions, the 60 New York and 180 Indiana drawings, in a more precise way. Consequently, we classified each of the drawings according to eight generally discernable dimensions: overall shape (scribbles, head only, head plus body, body parts, etc.), size, main color(s), hair length, hair color, hair style, characteristics of the head (eyes only, eyes plus mouth, etc.), and clothing. The characteristics were compared for the artist's grade and the intended sex of the figures. These cues then were subjected to a multiple regression analysis with modified dummy variables. A similar analysis was performed using the likelihood of recognition of the pictures as the basic data. The results of both analyses (Table 4.1) indicated that the three hair variables, but not clothing, contributed reliably to the prediction of the intended sex of the figures. For production of the drawings, the association of the hair variables with the intended sex of the figure was high (the multiple correlation coefficient, r, for the three variables was .70, accounting for 49% of the variance). Analyses of the standardized regression coefficients showed that although hair style correlated .45 with the intended gender of the figures, most of its contribution came from its association with hair length (.43) and hair color (.36). The standardized regression coefficients for hair color also declined from the simple coefficient with intended gender (.43) to .21 when its association with hair length (.32) was held constant. The results of the analysis on the recognition of drawings are summarized on the right side of Table 4.1.

If anything, the children's comments about how they knew the drawings were of a girl or a boy were even more interesting than their descriptions of

Table 4.1. **Multiple Regression Analyses of Drawings by Intended Gender**

Predictor Variables	Simple r	Multiple R	Standardized Regression Coefficient	Overall F	df
Hair length	.64	.64	.51	94.17***	1,133
Hair color	.43	.69	.21	58.43***	2,132
Hair style	.45	.70	.16	41.68***	3,131
R^2		.49			

*** $p < .001$

their own productions. Once again, hair assumed center stage, with hair length being mentioned more than the other characteristics. Curiously, children were not always consistent with their own ideas. For example, one preschooler happily classified a series of drawings with ambiguous hair by saying this one was a girl because it had long hair, the next one was a boy because it had short hair, and next one was a girl because it had short hair and girls sometimes have short hair, too. Another child announced that a drawing showed a boy because "girls don't have black hair." In another case, the drawing (Figure 4.4) had to be a girl, because it showed "a girl dancing and boys can't dance." It must be remembered that these sometimes disconcerting statements often accompanied accurate gender attribution and that the stated dependence on hair cues increased markedly from preschool to kindergarten, as did accurate gender attribution.

In general, kindergartners and third graders typically drew female figures with yellow hair that was at least chin length, and male figures with dark, shorter-than-chin length hair. Figures 4.2–4.3 show examples of preschoolers' drawings and Figures 4.4–4.6 present some of the kindergartners' drawings. Although the hair was sometimes depicted as straight for girls as well as boys, when the hair is drawn as curly or ponytailed, the intended gender was almost always female. Not one of the drawings depicted genitals or secondary sexual characteristics nor did any of our subjects mention these items.

Figure 4.2 Girl (left) and boy (right) drawn by a preschool boy.

Figure 4.3   Girl (left) and boy (right) drawn by a preschool girl.

Figure 4.4   Girl (left) and boy (right) drawn by a kindergarten boy.

Figure 4.5   Girl drawn by a kindergarten girl.

Figure 4.6   Boy drawn by the same kindergarten girl.

Concepts of Gender Constancy

We now turn to our second major concern, the question about the concepts of gender constancy. On the basis of previous work (Coker, 1984; Emmerich et al., 1977; Fagot, 1985; Marcus & Overton, 1978; Slaby & Frey, 1975), we expected to find the sequence: gender identity, temporal and situational gender constancy. The results corroborate this expectation, as shown in Table 4.2. Overall, 98% of the children identified their own gender, 73% correctly answered all of the temporal constancy questions (Questions 3–6, 11), and 58% correctly answered all of the situational constancy questions. We used a Guttman scale analysis (Anderson, 1966) to test the significance of these trends. For this analysis, a "passing" score of 1 was coded when subjects correctly answered all questions contributing to that measure; a "failing" score of 0 was coded if any errors were made. Because of the different numbers of questions contributing to each measure, "passing" scores were defined as two correct responses for gender identity, as five correct responses for temporal constancy, and as four correct responses for situational constancy. The Guttman analysis revealed reproducibility and scalability coefficients of .92 and .67, respectively, indicating that the scaled hierarchy is both valid and unidimensional. Moreover, the hierarchy occurred for all three grade levels (Table 4.2).

Two questions assessed the children's knowledge about whether or not they could change gender (motive). Eaton and Von Bargen (1981) and Emmerich et al. (1977) have contended that the concept that one cannot simply

Table 4.2.   Percentages of Subjects with Perfect Scores for the Measures of Gender Concepts

	Gender Identity	Temporal Gender Constancy	Situational Gender Constancy	Number of Children with Perfect Scores "Gender sophisticated"
Preschool	95	60	55	9
Kindergarten	100	85	55	10
Third Grade	100	80	65	10
Overall	98	73	58	

Rescaled Temporal Gender Constancy and Motive Classification

	Gender Identity	Temporal Gender Constancy	Motive (change gender at will)	Situational Gender Constancy
Preschool	95	90	60	55
Kindergarten	100	90	85	55
Third Grade	100	100	80	65

change gender at will (motive) is intermediate to gender stability (temporal gender constancy) and situational gender constancy. Accordingly, we re-scaled temporal constancy, using only responses to Questions 3–5 and re-assigned responses to Questions 6 and 11 to the new category of motive. The results of these changes appear in the lower panel of Table 4.2. A Guttman analysis yielded reproducibility and scalability coefficients of .95 and .71, respectively. These results suggest at least four components of gender concepts: knowledge of one's own gender, knowledge that one had that gender as a baby and will retain it as an adult, knowledge that one's gender cannot be changed at will, and—the last to develop—knowledge that gender remains invariant across different situations.

In addition to the above analyses, the internal consistency of the various temporal, motivational, and situational constancy measures was assessed by calculating Kuder-Richardson coefficients separately for each grade for each measure. The coefficients indicated satisfactory internal consistency.

Finally, we studied the responses for evidence of a clear understanding of gender constancy. As noted by Eaton & Von Bargen (1981), Emmerich et al., (1977), and Wehren and De Lisi (1983), children may make a correct answer on gender constancy questions and yet be unable to provide a reasonable explanation for their answer. Similarly, Kessler and McKenna (1978) reported that children's explanations of their gender attributions were often tautological and inadequate in other ways. We probed both phenomena by constantly asking the children to explain their choices. In both spheres, seemingly unrelated, indefensible, illogical reasons were often given for their answers.

Let us begin with the gender constancy questions. Of the 60% of pre-schoolers who answered the temporal gender constancy questions correctly, some 50% were unable to offer a reasonable explanation. Instead, they proposed irrelevant explanations such as "Because."

In contrast, kindergartners and third graders offered clear explanations about temporal gender constancy, often using words similar to those used by adults: "If people are born one sex, they stay that same sex the rest of their lives." These children also understand about motive constancy and situational gender constancy, indicating that people are not able to change their sex, even if they want to do so, and that their sex remains the same regardless of what clothes they wear, what activities they pursue, and so forth.

These results support those of Eaton and Von Bargen (1981), Emmerich et al. (1977), and Wehren and De Lisi (1983) by indicating that pseudocon-stancy is prevalent among three-year-olds but that it decreases markedly in kindergarten and the elementary school years. These investigators did not relate their findings with respect to the gender constancies to gender attri-bution, as we planned to do. We turn next to that analysis.

Gender Attribution and Gender Constancy

Children seem to acquire gender concepts in the order of gender identity, temporal gender constancy, motivational, and situational gender constancy. But are these concepts related to the ability to distinguish between the two sexes? Are children who answer correctly questions about gender constancy more sensitive to gender-differentiating cues than children who manifest fewer concepts of gender constancy? For one analysis, we divided each grade into two "gender sophistication" groups: the sophisticated group (with all correct answers on the 11 gender identity-constancy questions) and the less sophisticated group (with one or more errors on the gender identity-constancy questions). Table 4.2 shows that approximately half of the children at each grade were classified as gender-sophisticated. This variable was part of the three analyses of variance (New York, Indiana, and own drawings) described above.

All analyses showed that the gender-sophisticated and less gender-sophisticated subjects made approximately the same numbers of correct gender attributions for all three sets of drawings. In brief, sophistication with gender concepts had no effect on gender attribution.

This tentative conclusion of nonassociation between gender attribution of children's drawings and gender constancy is further supported by the low and nonsigificant correlations (.05 and .10 for the New York and Indiana drawings) between gender attributions and the total scores on the gender constancy questions. As previously noted, both gender constancy scores and gender attribution performance are internally consistent and reliable, hence the failure to find an interaction between them would not arise from unreliability of the measures. It seems, then, that gender attribution and the gender constancies may be acquired independently, rather than sequentially, as predicted by Kohlberg's (1966) cognitive-developmental model.

Summing Up

Using children's drawings as the stimulus materials, we found converging patterns of cues by children to produce gender-differentiated pictures and to recognize the gender intended by other youthful artists. Children use hair length, color, and style as the major cues for identifying gender. This result was so surprising that we reanalyzed the results by sorting the data into categories based on the child's own hair cues. These cues made no difference. For example, blond-haired, curly-headed boys were just as likely to indicate that boys had dark, straight hair as dark, straight-haired boys. Moreover, minority children also made the same kinds of differentiations.

The importance of both hair color and hair style appears to have been overlooked when adults selected the cues to be tested (e.g., Conn, 1940; Katcher,

1955; Levin et al., 1972; McConaghy, 1979; Thompson, 1975; Thompson & Bentler, 1971). Our children did not rely on size, body contours, or genitalia (none of the children drew genitals or secondary sexual characteristics)— cues that adults may use (Kessler & McKenna, 1978; Thompson & Bentler, 1971). In fact, hair length was the only major gender cue for children identified by both our child-referenced materials and adult-selected ones, with clothing as a secondary cue. In addition, we found no evidence for special sensitivity to gender cues associated with the child's own sex.

The results speak to some of the predictions listed in Chapter 3. For example, we found no support for the Freudian prediction that physical genitalia should be the most important gender markers for children. Not only were genitals not the most important gender cues, genitals did not appear to be used at all by our young subjects. Neither did we find evidence that even the youngest children identified female drawings more readily than male drawings as implied by Chodorow's (1976) version of psychoanalytic theory. To the contrary, the children seemed to find it equally easy to identify male and female figures, suggesting that they had schemata for both genders.

Cognitive developmental theory fared a little better, in the sense that children showed the expected developmental trend of gender identity, then temporal gender constancy, and situational gender constancy. This developmental trend did not predict accurate gender attribution, however. Thus, it seems that gender concepts of identity and the constancies are acquired independently of gender differentiators. This would not be surprising, since the gender concepts are not necessarily linked with the kinds of cues used to separate people into two gender classes. One other result was inconsistent with a cognitive developmental perspective: The children did not use size as a gender marker.

According to both Kessler and McKenna's (1978) cultural genital model and our cultural gender model male-related cues should be preeminent. Once again, the data were contradictory, for male- and female-related cues were equally salient across all three age groups and for both sexes. Thus, at least through the third grade, female gender concepts appear to be as well developed as male gender concepts.

The finding shed some light on the contents of these concepts by showing the order of acquiring the concepts of gender identity and constancy and the independence of these concepts from gender attribution performance. The findings do not illuminate other likely components of children's gender concepts, such as traits, activities, behaviors, and the like.

The results cannot be used to evaluate the social learning theory or the gender schema models, because no information is available about reinforcement histories or about the contents of their gender schemata in the senses used by these models.

These results surprised us, and we decided to explore possible reasons for them. One explanation was that the children had been exposed to the same books in the preschool and that these books showed blond, curly-headed girls (Goldilocks, perhaps) and dark, straight-haired boys. So, we systematically examined the 34 books owned by the school. The hair length, color, and style of the main character and of all major characters in each book were tallied as functions of the sex of the character. These efforts were for naught, as far as an explanation was concerned, for the two sexes were depicted almost identically with respect to hair characteristics (although the boys tended to be portrayed in adventurous, exciting roles and the girls, if any were present, in supportive, home-related activities).

The next possibility was the local municipal library, since there was no way to visit the homes of each of the children. We enlisted the help of a local librarian to identify the 66 most popular children's books. Popularity was defined by the frequency of borrowing the books. We applied the same procedure—with the same results. The books portrayed the sexes in markedly gender-stereotypic ways (e.g., McArthur & Eisen, 1976; Weitzman et al., 1972), but differential treatments of hair and other physical characteristics are not among them. Thus, among a total of 100 books we found astonishing evidence of differential portrayals of the two sexes, but hair characteristics did not distinguish between the sexes.

We turned to the next most obvious source: television. We studied all of the late afternoon programs aimed at children and Saturday morning features on the three major networks and the Public Broadcasting Service for four weeks, using our standard system of scoring hair and physical characteristics of the main and major actors. This time we were successful. Indeed, we were successful beyond our wildest imagination. In almost every case when a program had both sexes of characters (85% of the 199 programs analyzed), the hair color of females was lighter than that of males. Similarly, females' hair was more likely to be curly, whereas males' hair was more likely to be straight. Of 245 females, 240 had curly or pigtailed hair. Of 305 males, 300 had straight hair. The figures were almost the same for hair length: 241 of the females had hair that was longer than chin-length; 303 of the males had hair that was chin-length or shorter.

Most surprising of all, when programs about animals were considered, the figures rose even higher. For example, for the programs with both sexes of animals, the females *always* had lighter fur (or feathers) than the males.

Interesting as these explorations were, they could not tell us about the true origins of the salient use of hair cues to attribute gender. The most that we could hope to do was to identify areas to examine more systematically in later research.

At this point we turned our attention back to the challenging question of whether or not our young artists had identified the most important indicators of gender attribution. Overall, our youthful subjects relied mainly on three hair cues to distinguish gender—a surprising result, both because none of the hair cues is a particularly reliable discriminator and because the number of cues is limited. The regression analysis suggested that hair length is the single most important cue, followed by hair color, and hair style. These differentiators all were identified in the children's drawings, and thus are child-produced and child-recognized cues. Despite the usefulness of this approach as the first part of our project, we now had to ask how effective each of these cues would be in more controlled situations. After all, each of the hair cues is a fallible predictor. Would hair length be the controlling cue if the hair color and hair style of a stimulus figure were contradictory? For example, if a figure has one male-associated cue, say short hair, and two female-associated cues, say blond, curly hair, would children identify the figure as a boy or a girl? Questions like these motivated additional research.

CHAPTER 5

Relative Importance of Hair and Clothing Cues in Children's Gender Attribution

Child: I can't do it. I can't tell if it is a boy or a girl.

Experimenter: Why not?

Child: Because I can't see the hair. If you don't show me the hair, how can I tell if it is a boy or a girl?

As we have seen, when children draw pictures of girls and boys they rely primarily on hair length, hair color, hair style, and occasionally clothing to distinguish between the sexes. These same cues are used by other children to identify the intended gender of the drawings. These drawings enabled the children to show us some gender markers that were important to them, but they did not tell us how effective combinations of the cues would be when children had to identify gender. For example, they did not indicate how many characteristics usually associated with females (or males) had to be present before most children labeled the drawing as that of a female (or male). These issues prompted the next two experiments.

Picture Experiment

In the "picture" experiment, we wanted to vary the hair length, color, and style, and the clothing of children in specially prepared pictures so that the contribution of single and multiple cues could be assessed. Thus, we prepared pictures that illustrated combinations of hair length (shorter-than-chin length and longer-than-chin length), hair color (light and dark), hair style (straight or curled at the end), and clothing (unisex or sex-typed). The challenge with this situation was to find a task that enlisted the interest and the cooperation of preschoolers, whose attention spans are notoriously short. After some pretesting, we decided to use a hand puppet (a fuzzy, nondescript animal). We told the children that the puppet had come from a faraway land and was very curious about lots of things here in this country. The puppet had been asking us so many questions that we were a little tired. We needed some help—that was why we were asking the children to help us answer some of the puppet's questions. At the moment, the puppet wanted to know whether the children in some pictures were girls or boys...

Thus, the tasks of our preschool subjects were to tell a puppet from a far-away land whether each child in the pictures was a girl or boy and to name each of the depicted children. The latter (naming) task probed the ability of preschoolers to use gender-stereotyped names. To our knowledge, this ability has not been tested previously, although it has obvious cognitive implications for categorizing people by gender. If the children's gender concepts contain first names, then they should be able to consistently assign girls' names to the pictures of people they identified as girls and boys' names to the pictures of people they called boys. Their ability to make consistent assignments would indicate that they recognized the gender assignments of the names and were able to apply them appropriately by the time they were three years of age.

If the various characteristics of hair or clothing are reliable indicators of gender for young children, our respondents should assign both gender labels and gender-stereotyped names above a chance level. This approach also permitted us to ascertain the relative weights of each of the cues. Further, if our previous data are reconfirmed, figures with blond hair are likely to be labeled female. Suppose a "masculine" characteristic, say short hair, is combined with blondness. Will the gender attribution change? Will the gender attribution change to a greater extent if the hair has two "masculine" characteristics such as shortness and straightness? In brief, our design studied the effects of individual cues and their combinations on gender attribution.

We sought stimulus materials that met three requirements: They should portray interesting activities to attract the children's attention and assistance; they should show activities that were attractive to both sexes so that the nature of the activities would not include a bias in gender attribution; and they should be easily modified to represent our three hair and clothing characteristics. Luckily, we found two children's picture books that were ideal, Mircea Vasiliu's *A Day at the Beach* and Patricia Thackeray's *Raggedy Ann at the Carnival*.

The next task was to select pictures of four children engaged in four different activities. We chose two from each book. The four activities, building sand castles or jumping from rock to rock at the water's edge (from the *Beach* book) and riding either a roller coaster or a merry-go-round (from the *Carnival* book), are shown in Figures 5.1–5.4.

Figure 5.1 Sample stimulus scene showing children in sex-typed clothes building a sand castle.

Figure 5.2 Sample stimulus scene showing children in unisex clothes playing on rocks.

Figure 5.3 Sample stimulus scene showing children in unisex clothes on roller coaster.

Figure 5.4 Sample stimulus scene showing children in sex-typed clothes on a merry-go-round.

After copying these scenes, we systematically varied the hair and clothing characteristics. This involved combining one level of each of the three hair variables with one level of the clothing variable. Specifically, the basic design called for using all eight combinations of the three hair variables, length, color, and style, with either unisex clothing (shorts and T-shirts) or with sex-typed clothing (dresses or trousers and shirts). The eight combinations of hair variables were those constructed from the two levels of hair length (longer-than-chin length, L1; shorter-than-chin length, L2), hair color (blond, C1; black, C2), and hair style (curled at end, S1; and straight, S2). Note that the above abbreviations are defined as follows: L = length, C = color, S = style, 1 = female-associated cue, and 2 = male-associated cue. Thus, an L1-C1-S1 figure had three female-associated hair cues (longer-than-chin length, blond hair that was curled at the ends), whereas an L2-C2-S2 figure had three male-associated hair cues (shorter-than-chin length, dark, straight hair). To repeat, the eight possible combinations of hair cues were used. We treated the drawings portraying these eight children as a set. All children in one set were depicted in unisex clothing (shorts and T-shirts).

A second set of drawings showed four children in either the other beach scene (jumping from rock to rock along the water's edge) or four children on another amusement park ride (the merry-go-round). All children in this set were dressed in sex-typed clothing (sex-typed swimming suits in the beach scene; dresses or shorts and trousers in the amusement park). The third and fourth sets of drawings reversed the sex-typing of the clothing. Thus, the third set showed children building the sand castle while wearing sex-typed bathing suits, and the children on the roller coaster wearing dresses or trousers. The fourth set used unisex clothing for the two other scenes. Hence, over the four sets, the factorial combinations of the hair were combined with each level of clothing. The pictures then were encased in plastic so they could be handed to the children.

We tested 18 children (eight girls and ten boys) from a local preschool. Their ages ranged from three to six years, with a mean of 4.5 years. Approximately even numbers of children were assigned to combinations of the four sets of stimulus pictures.

Two experimenters worked as a pair. They introduced the children to the puppet saying that the puppet, "Camby," was from a far away place. Camby had just come to town and was very interested in knowing about people in our country. The experimenters had pictures that showed some of the things Camby was curious about. The experimenters wanted the child to give them some help explaining to Camby whether the pictures showed girls or boys. Camby also wanted to know the children's names. Each subject then was shown the first picture and asked whether the child in the picture was a girl or a boy (the order of citing the two sexes was random, but equal overall) and the child's name. This procedure continued until the child had assigned gender to two sets of pictures (16 pictured children). They were then asked how they knew the children were girls or boys.

Next, each child was asked 12 questions about gender concepts, four assessing gender identity, four testing temporal gender constancy (two of which tested motive), and four testing situational gender constancy. These questions were the same as those used for the drawing experiment except that two more gender identity items were added. ("Does your mother call you a girl or a boy?" and "Does your mother call you a [opposite sex of first response]?"). These changes were made to equalize the number of questions contributing to each general category of gender concepts.

Potency of Single and Multiple Hair Cues as Gender Differentiators

If the cues from the children's drawings are indeed reliable gender differentiators for children, than hair characteristics should predict the genders assigned to our stimulus figures. And that is exactly what we found (Table 5.1). When the hair was longer than chin length, 94% of the figures were labeled girls. When the hair was blond, 74% of the figures were called girls, and when the hair was curled at the ends, 69% of the figures were called girls. These percentages of classification as girls exceeded chance beyond the .001 level for all three hair characteristics. Hair length also reliably predicted labeling figures as males: When the hair was shorter than chin length, 73% of the figures were called boys. Neither dark hair (47%) nor straight hair (52%) reliably signified males. Thus, only hair length, taken alone, predicts maleness, whereas all three hair cues, taken singly, can be used to predict femaleness. These results replicate the central findings of our experiment with children's drawings. In addition, they suggest that the hair characteristics associated with females are more potent predictors of gender attribution than the hair characteristics associated with males.

Table 5.1.   Probability of Saying "Girl" or "Boy" as Functions of Hair Characteristics

Hair Characteristics	Girl	Boy
Length		
Long	.94***	.06***
Short	.27***	.73***
Color		
Yellow	.73***	.26***
Black	.53	.47
Style		
Curly	.69***	.31***
Straight	.52	.48

*** Probability differs from chance at .001 level.

We turn next to combinations of the hair cues. Figure 5.5 plots the percentages of labeling the figures as girls or boys as functions of combinations of the various hair characteristics and the clothing. Figure 5.5 indicates that figures are likely to be called girls if the hair is at least chin length regardless of the other characteristics. If the hair is short but has two other "female" characteristics (blonde and curled at the ends), the figure is also likely to be labeled female. Only if the hair is shorter than chin length *and* has at least one other "masculine" characteristic (dark color or straight) is the figure labeled as male beyond a chance level. One gets the impression that the protocol for maleness has strict, rigid boundaries. If the result of this check fails to yield male characteristics the figure is assigned to the larger, "other," category of female.

Potency of Clothing Cues as Gender Differentiators

How important are clothing cues? Clothing cues were not very important in this experiment, although they were in the work of Katcher (1955) and others. These results replicated those of our first experiment. As Figure 5.5 indicates, clothes become important only when a masculine hair length (short) and one other masculine hair cue (either straight or black hair) are combined with one feminine cue (color or style). In these cases, figures with trousers are called boys and figures with dresses are called girls. Figures in unisex clothing are called boys about as often as they are called girls. It seems, then, that when the hair is long (feminine-associated length), the figure is called a girl, regardless of the other hair cues or the clothing cues. When the hair is short, black, and straight (all three masculine-associated cues), the

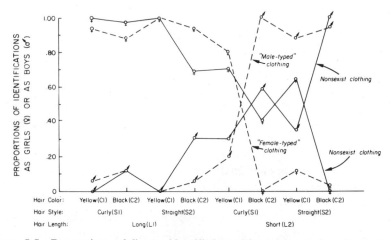

Figure 5.5 **Proportions of figures identified as girls or boys as functions of hair length, hair style, hair color, and clothing.**

figure is called a boy, regardless of its clothes. Only when at least one feminine-associated cue is combined with short hair does clothing affect gender
attribution. Clothing clearly operates as a minor gender marker. Once
again, we see that the cues associated with boyness are both limited and
rigid compared to those associated with girlness.

This conclusion was further supported by additional analyses. Long hair
was associated 61 times with figures called girls; short hair was associated
with figures called boys 24 times. This is true despite the fact that the two
sexes were represented equally often in the drawings. When explaining why
figures with long hair had been called boys, two children volunteered that,
"Some boys have long hair," or "He didn't get his hair cut." No comparable explanations were given for short-haired figures that were called girls.
Curly hair was mentioned 24 times for figures called girls; it was mentioned
only once for figures called boys. Moreover, straight hair was never cited as
a cue for males, suggesting that the major hair style differentiator was the
presence (= female) or absence (= male) of curly hair.

Gender-typing of Names

As part of their knowledge about gender differentiation, preschool children
may have information about the gender-typing of names. We examined
whether the name assigned to each pictured figure was stereotypically used
for the gender the child had assigned to the figure. Not all children gave
names to all figures. Of those who did, the names were stereotypically
related to the gender assigned to the pictured figure 100% of the time. Obviously, these preschool children had learned the gender-typing of first names
and they used these names in correspondence with cultural stereotypes.

Gender Concepts

All of our respondents showed gender identity. That is, all of them correctly
answered each of the four questions about their own gender identity. All
but two respondents also answered correctly all questions about temporal
gender constancy and the two missed one question each. The missed questions all assessed knowledge that one could not voluntarily change gender
(motive). Our respondents, then, knew they were a particular gender and
that one's gender typically remains constant over time. They were considerably less aware that gender remains constant even if one wears clothes or
plays games usually associated with the other sex. The mean number of the
situational gender constancy questions answered correctly was 1.94—about
half of them. Most respondents made some errors; four respondents made
none. The pattern of gender constancy corresponds to what we found in the
drawing experiment of gender identity, temporal, motivational and then
situational gender constancy. A Guttman scale analysis, performed to

assess the significance of the trends, yielded reproducibility and scalability coefficients of .95 and .74, respectively, indicating that the hierarchy is valid and unidimensional. For this analysis, a "passing" score of 1 was recorded when subjects correctly answered all four questions contributing to that measure; a "failing" score of 0 was recorded if any errors were made.

Again, we found substantial evidence of pseudoconstancy: More than 50% of the youngsters who responded correctly to the gender constancy questions were unable to explain the basis for their answer in a manner that indicated understanding of the basic concepts.

Clearly, then, although our preschool respondents were aware of their own gender identities and the temporal permanence of these identities, many had doubts about the constancy of gender when clothes and play activities shifted to those often associated with the other sex. To the extent that these doubts reflect some fragility of the concepts of gender, the children making errors on the situational gender questions might respond to the hair and clothing cues in a more random fashion than the children who made no errors on the situational gender questions. To test this possibility, we contrasted the performance of the respondents who missed at least one of these questions with that of the four children who made no errors. The overall patterns of labeling did not differ. Hence, these results do not support the position that children with fragile concepts of situational gender constancy will be less sensitive to gender-related cues than children with greater understanding of situational gender constancy.

Summing Up

In general, these results support and extend those from the experiment with children's drawings. Consistent with Brieland and Nelson (1951), we found that hair cues are particularly important gender cues for children. The children in the picture experiment were likely to label figures with long, curly, yellow hair as female and those with short, straight, dark hair as male. When the figures have hair characteristics associated with more than one gender, the probability that the figure was labeled as female (or male) decreased, suggesting that children use cues in a combinatorial fashion, although female-associated cues seem to be a broader class than male-associated hair cues. The reasons stated for deciding about the gender of the figure tended to correspond to the manipulated hair variables, and the names attached were systematically stereotypic of the gender label given to the figure.

Before considering the implications of these results, we wished to test more naturalistic cues, both to increase the generality of the results and to explore the possibilities that certain dynamic cues, such as posture and activity, also contribute to gender attribution. Consequently, our next experiment used videotapes of children as the stimulus materials.

Figure 5.6   Gender is difficult to identify, with certainty, when hair and clothing cues are obscured.

Videotape Experiment I

Suppose children are videotaped with their hair covered and these videotapes are then presented to other children for gender attributions. Will the absence of hair cues retard gender attribution? Figure 5.6 gives an example of how important these—and perhaps, clothing—cues can be. Can you state their gender? With certainty? If the children were moving you might have more clues to their gender. This picture, and the stimuli used in the drawing and picture experiments, are static and artificial. Such stimuli exclude potentially important dynamic cues associated with real people. To study dynamic cues, we turned to videotapes of moving preschool children. These materials also let us focus on more naturalistic stimuli. Our plan was to videotape children at one nursery school, using various disguises to conceal certain cues, and to then show these videotapes to children at a different preschool in another section of the city. The task of the children at the second school was to identify the gender of the filmed models.

The children at the first school were taped in conditions designed to systematically exclude certain cues. In the first condition, the children were videotaped in regular play clothes. This procedure was planned to capture an extensive range of cues other children and adults might use as gender differentiators. In a second condition, the children wore capes over their clothing to exclude clothing cues. In this condition, then, cues from hair characteristics, posture, activity, and the like remain intact while those from clothing are eliminated. In the third condition, the children donned paper bag hoods in addition to the capes before being taped. (The taping was done just before Halloween so the children readily accepted wearing the capes and hoods.) This combination excluded clothing, hair, and other head cues. Presumably, only dynamic cues such as posture, gait, activity, would mediate gender attribution in this condition.

All of the children were taped in one condition before the next condition was filmed. The hair characteristics for the fourteen videotaped children (Table 5.2) cover the range found in the drawing experiment. In addition, two girls were wearing dresses and one other girl wore a skirt and blouse. All other children were wearing shirts and pants. The tapes were visual only because the microphones were turned off to eliminate auditory input.

Table 5.2.   Hair Characteristics of Videotaped Children, Frequencies of Using Gender Labels, and the Rank Order Correlation Between These Variables

| Gender Attribution | | | | | Subjects[a] | |
| | | | | | Preschool | | Adults | |
Length	Hair Style	Color	Female	Male	Female	Male
Videotaped Girls						
Long[b]	Curly	Blonde	12	8	12	12
Long[b]	Braided	Blonde	10	10	12	12
Long[c]	Straight	Dark	11	9	12	12
Short[d]	Curly	Blonde	12	10	12	12
Mid-ear	Straight	Blonde	8	5	6	9
Mid-ear	Straight	Dark	5	9	2	5
Mid-ear	Straight	Dark	8	6	1	4	overall
Rank order correlations (N = 7)			.74	.41	.90	.90	.74
p			.029	.183	.003	.000	.030
Videotaped Boys						
Short	Straight	Dark	11	12	11	12
Short	Straight	Blonde	12	12	12	12
Short	Straight	Light brown	11	12	12	12
Mid-ear	Straight	Blonde	11	11	10	10
Long	Curly	Dark	10	8	6	9
Mid-ear	Curly	Blonde	10	10	11	11
Long	Straight	Blonde	9	11	10	10
Rank order correlations (N = 7)			.88	.77	.57	.73	.76
p			.005	.023	.092	.032	.025

[a] Maximum number of attributions = 12
[b] Wearing a dress
[c] Wearing a skirt and blouse
[d] All other children wore T-shirts and pants

These videotaped figures were the stimuli of the gender attribution task. Twenty four children aged three to six from a different preschool served as subjects. Two of the preschool subjects were Black and one was Hispanic. Then, to extend our results to an older age range, 24 college students aged 18 to 20 were tested, as well. Four of the college students were Black. Half of each age group was female and half was male. Four females and four males from each age group were assigned to each of the three orders of viewing the conditions (regular clothes, wearing capes, wearing capes and hoods). Hence, all subjects saw all three conditions, but the order of viewing the conditions was balanced across age groups and the gender of the respondents.

The subjects' task was to identify the gender of the videotaped persons. The cover task of telling a puppet from a faraway land about people here was again used with the preschoolers.

Attributing Gender When Hair and Clothing Cues Are or Are Not Obscured

Of central importance is the accuracy of gender attribution under the three conditions of videotaping. We predicted that accuracy would decline when hair cues were covered by paper bag hoods, but not when clothing cues were eliminated by capes. Before we could answer this question, we needed to find out if the subjects showed a tendency to guess one sex more often than the other, regardless of the gender of the pictured child. That is, the subjects might show a "bias" toward guessing one sex more than the other, as Kessler and McKenna (1978) observed. Like them, we did, indeed, find such a bias, with boys being guessed more than girls across all stimulus figures. Preschool boys were particularly prone to guess "boy" more than "girl."

To eliminate this response bias, we needed a technique that would enable us to compare correct identifications of gender (so-called "hits," because they are assumed to reflect the likelihood of saying "girl" or "boy" when the participant knows the sex label to be given to the child) with incorrect identifications of gender (so-called "false alarms," because these responses are assumed to reflect a general bias toward saying one sex or the other when the participant is guessing). The statistic we chose, A', provides such an estimate.[1] With A', if a respondent always gives the same answer (boy or girl), regardless of the stimulus figure, A' would be .5, its lowest possible value. Thus, A' is a measure of the ability of the respondents to make dis-

---

[1] A' computes the area under a receiver-operating-characteristic (ROC) curve using the formula $.5 + ((1 - F + H)/4) \times ((H - F)/H - (H \times F))$, where H = proportion of hits (correct identifications of gender) and F = proportion of false alarms (incorrect identification of gender). A' does not assume that the variances of the distributions of hits and false alarms are normally and equally distributed.

criminating choices. Accordingly, we calculated A′ scores for each subject for each condition. These scores, depicted in Figure 5.7, indicate that the accuracy of attributing gender cues was high for both age groups in the two conditions that left hair cues unobscured, but when the filmed children wore paper bag hoods and capes, accuracy dropped to chance level for both age groups and for both genders of subjects. The main effect for condition was reliable, $F(2, 44) = 66.92$, $p < .01$, and did not interact with age group, $F(2, 44) = 1.85$, $p > .05$. Hence, the pattern of responding to the three conditions was highly similar for both age groups.

The chance level of responding when hair and head cues were excluded was particularly interesting because it suggests that the dynamic cues remaining in this condition were not powerful enough to support accurate gender labeling. We are left with hair—and possibly head—cues as highly important markers of the gender of preschoolers. Moreover, these hair cues are just as important gender markers for adults as they are for children. These intriguing results imply that gender cues do not necessarily lose their effectiveness as people age. Rather, other cues, such as genitals and secondary sexual characteristics may become more important over time, perhaps because they are perceived as more reliable, more valid, or more essential. It is even quite possible that adults are not aware of all the cues that they do use, either singly or in combination, to identify gender.

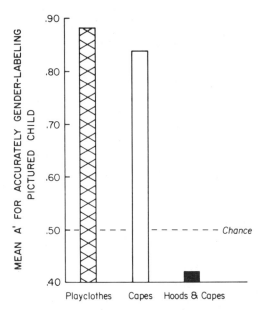

Figure 5.7 A′ scores for accurately identifying gender when children were videotaped wearing regular clothes, cape over their clothes, or paper bag masks plus capes.

Attributing Gender with Different Combinations of Hair Cues

We turn next to the question of how the hair characteristics of the filmed children affected the accuracy of gender attribution. To perform this analysis, we first tabulated the hair of the filmed children in terms of the three types of hair cues. Then, using the data of the picture experiment as the basis, we were able to predict the likelihood that each videotaped child would be labeled a girl or a boy. The rank orders of these predictions then were tested against the ranks of the actual frequencies of labeling female children as girls and male children as boys in the regular play clothes condition. The Spearman rank order correlation coefficients and their probabilities appear in Table 5.2. Although the number of pairs (7) is small in each case, the pattern of the correlation coefficients is clear. Overall, the correlations were positive, indicating that knowledge of the hair characteristics improved the likelihood of accurately identifying the gender of the videotaped children, and this improvement was statistically significant when all respondents were taken into account (the overall rank order correlation for correctly identifying videotaped girls, given hair cues, was .74, $p = .030$, and the counterpart coefficient for videotaped boys was .76, $p = .025$). There were some minor, but interesting deviations from the general pattern: Preschool males and adult females did not show statistically significant correlations, although their coefficients were in the expected direction. These results suggest that the accuracy of gender attribution can be quite precisely predicted from the natural characteristics of the hair alone.

This consideration of the natural variations in hair characteristics of the filmed children also offers a possible explanation for the bias toward labeling the children as males. Of the 14 stimulus children, nine had shorter-than-chin length hair, nine had straight hair, and six had light brown and dark hair. Thus of the 42 hair cues (14 children × 3 hair variables) 24 or 57% were associated with males. These hair cues might have induced the subjects to label the figures as boys or, as Kessler and McKenna suggest, the result may reflect a cultural and social preeminence of males.

Summing Up

What have we learned about gender differentiators so far? Clearly, characteristics of hair are so important to the accurate gender attribution of videotaped preschool children that when these cues are concealed, gender attribution by both adults and other preschoolers declines to a chance level. These results suggest that such dynamic cues as gait, posture, and activity are not used to identify gender at least for our videotaped stimulus persons.

When hair cues are present, they serve as markers of the gender of children. This is true for schematic drawings, for pictures, and for videotapes of children. Long hair, curly (ponytailed, braided) hair, and blond hair are associated more often with females; short hair, straight hair, and dark hair, with males. Of the two sets of cues, those associated with males appear to be more limited and rigid, almost as though the credentials for admission to the "boy" club were simultaneously more constrained and more constraining than those more numerous ones defining the "girl" club. Indeed, our data to date could be interpreted as suggesting that the absence of female-associated hair characteristics increases the likelihood that the stimulus will be called a boy. Boys can't have many girl-related cues if they are to be called boys.

This latter result is a fascinating one, for it lends support to the contention that, at least during childhood, a central concept of male gender roles is defined as a negative contrast with females: Males should not be like females (David & Brannon, 1976; Farrell, 1974; Hartley, 1959; Pleck, 1981). This view is further bolstered by some of the reasons children stated for the labels they assigned to the stimulus figures.

Last, hair style is a potent gender marker; nevertheless, its effectiveness stems in part from its association with hair length. When hair is very short, any curliness is less likely to be apparent than when the hair is long. Hair color also was correlated with hair length and hair style in the drawing experiment, although the bases for these associations are obscure.

Videotape Experiment II

Dynamic gender cues did not affect the accuracy of gender attribution with the videotaped children in the last experiment. These cues were limited to a few brief activities, and the taped sequences may have been too short to permit the subjects to follow and evaluate the activities. This possibility seems particularly likely for older subjects, because gender distinctions about activity seem to be made regularly. Consider sitting, for example. As Henley (1977) comments, women tend to occupy relatively little space, sitting in a scrunched position with their arms and legs close to the body. Men are more likely to sprawl over a chair, with both arms and legs distended from the body, often draped over a chair.

Moreover, undergraduates can accurately identify the gender of female and male undergraduate walkers about 60-65% of the time from films of the light patterns reflected from reflecting tape attached to the walkers' joints (Barclay, Cutting, & Kozlowski, 1978; Cutting & Kozlowski, 1977), although gender recognition drops to chance for static patterns (Kozlowski & Cutting, 1977). Frykholm (1983a, 1983b) also reported that 11-year-olds' gender recognition of the light patterns of walkers was about the same as that of adults, and Runeson and Frykholm (1983) found even higher gender recognition (75%) when adults and 11- or 12-year-olds of both sexes were photographed performing a series of actions (including walking, sitting, running, carrying a box, picking up and throwing an eraser). These experiments typically used adult observers to judge side views of adult performers. These results indicate that various postural cues merit investigation. So, too, does language, or the voice. Most of the time, we hear others in our environment, and these oral cues may signal their owners' gender.

The last experiment in this series tested various dynamic cues, or what the anthropologist Birdwhistell (1970) called *tertiary* sexual characteristics (primary characteristics refer to the physiology in ova and sperm production, and secondary characteristics to anatomical sexual attributes). Birdwhistell also emphasizes postural and other kinds of communication cues.

Once again, we were faced with the dilemma of selecting the cues to be tested, knowing that this selection foreclosed the investigation of unchosen cues. We decided to test activities that we see most often—the kinds of activities that may well govern our gender attributions, even from a distance. Hence, with some trepidation, we chose standing, running, sitting, walking, and talking. Other concerns nagged at us: What about other "static" cues, such as faces, apart from hair cues? In the last video study, the paper bag masks hid facial cues in addition to hair characteristics, but when hair cues were present faces were shown, as well. In short, hair and facial cues were confounded. The time had come to unconfound them, so in this experiment the models performed the various activities with or without their hair obscured by shower caps. The models wore unisex clothing part of the time and sex-typed clothing the rest of the time. The final innovation of this experiment was to test models of differing ages, instead of only the preschoolers we used in the last study. This procedure gave us the opportunity to map developmental trends in the use of various gender cues for both the observed stimulus persons and the observers. We could ascertain whether or not specific gender cues change in potency as the age of the model increases and whether these cues change as the age of the subject-observer increases.

In this experiment, we did not systematically vary the three types of hair cues, except for the present-versus-shower-cap-concealed manipulation. To recapitulate, the following cues were varied:

1. *Activity.* The models sat, walked, ran, stood silently, or stood while they spoke two standardized sentences.
2. *Hair cues.* The above activities were performed with the hair uncovered and with the hair tucked into a shower cap.
3. *Clothing cues.* The above activities were performed while dressed in unisex clothing (jeans or shorts and a baggy shirt) and while dressed in sex-typed clothing (skirt or dress for females, pants and tucked-in shirt for males).
4. *Front or back view.* The above activities were taped from both front and rear views.

These variables yielded a total of 40 sequences that were performed by each of 32 models as we videotaped them. In addition to the above potential cues, the age and sex of the models and of the subjects varied.

5. *Models' age and sex.* The models were four females and four males at each of four age groups: three-, eight-, 14-year-olds, and 18-year-old college students. The adult males were smoothly shaven.

6. *Subjects' age and sex.* The 96 subjects were 12 females and 12 males at each of the same four age groups as the models, three-, eight-, 14-year-olds, and 18-year-old college students.

The combinations of 32 models performing each of 40 sequences yielded 1280 sequences to be judged, too large and unwieldy a number to inflict on a single subject. Consequently, we generated 16 test films, each containing 80 randomly sampled and randomly ordered sequences. The sampling was restricted to minimize the number of times any one model appeared. These films were assigned randomly to each sex and age group of subjects, with the restriction that each tape be used with approximately equal frequency. As with our earlier work, the subject's task was to watch the stimulus sequence and to then indicate whether the featured person was a girl (woman) or a boy (man).

Attributing Gender from Activities with Static Cues Controlled

The results were straightforward, despite the complexity of the design. To analyze them, we began with the dynamic cues since they were the special interest in this experiment. Our initial approach was to hold other factors as constant as possible while studying the effects of the dynamic cues (standing, sitting, walking, running, talking) on accurate gender identification. Hence, we first examined the dynamic cues when the hair cues were covered, the models were dressed in unisex clothing, and the camera shots were of the model's back (see Figure 5.8). Under these conditions, the dynamic cues afforded accurate gender identification only when the two older groups (14- and 18-years-olds) of subjects were judging the two similarly aged groups of models, results that are compatible with those of Cutting and his associates (Barclay et al., 1978; Cutting & Kozlowski, 1977; Cutting, Proffitt, & Kozlowski, 1978; Kozlowski & Cutting, 1977) and Runeson and Frykholm (1983). When the two younger groups of subjects, the 3- and 8-year-olds, saw the older stimulus persons engaged in the dynamic activities, they correctly identified the stimulus person's gender about half of the time—that is, at a chance level. Further, none of the age groups of subjects was able to correctly identify the gender of younger models (aged three and eight) in the dynamic conditions. Finally, the above results were not qualified by the sex of either the subject or of the model. Thus, for the back view of hair-obscured

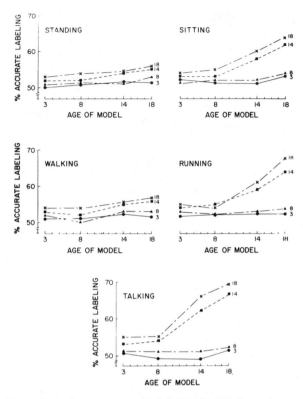

Figure 5.8 Percentage of accurate gender labeling for the dynamic cues from standing, sitting, walking, running, and talking when hair cues were obscured. The models were dressed in unisex clothing, and back views were shown.

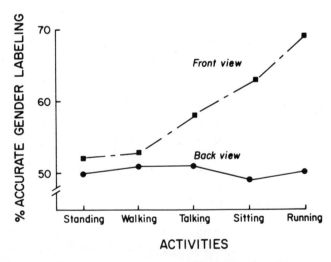

Figure 5.9 Percentage of accurate gender labeling for the dynamic cues from standing, sitting, walking, running, and talking comparing front and back views.

figures dressed in unisex clothing, the message is starkly clear: Gender information connoted by our dynamic cues does not effectively differentiate gender for either the sender or the receiver of this information until about the time of puberty.

In general, both front views and sex-typed clothing aid gender identification a small amount for all age groups and sexes of subjects, regardless of the age, sex, or dynamic activity of the stimulus person. Frontal views (including facial features, of course) and sex-typed clothing thus may help a little, but they do not appear to be major gender markers.

Attributing Gender from Static Cues with Activities Controlled

The major gender markers, even when the stimulus persons are engaging in various kinds of activities, were our old friends, the hair cues. To analyze these cues, we again catalogued the hair of the models by length, color, and style. And, as before, these cues were strongly associated with accurate gender identification, even for adult subjects judging adult models. Moreover, these cues interacted with the dynamic cues, and with the ages of the models and the subjects. As Table 5.3 expresses, when the hair cues are consistent with the model's gender (long, blond, curled hair for female models; short, dark, straight hair for male models) the percentages of correct gender attribution are the highest—particularly for the older age groups of subjects judging the two older age groups of running, sitting, and talking models. Inconsistent hair cues have the opposite effect—that of suppressing the percentages of correct gender identifications. The sex of the subject and of the model did not affect any of the above results.

So far, the results tell quite a simple story. When asked to judge the gender of clothed individuals, a common experience in our culture, hair characteristics seem to be important determinants for all ages and sexes. After puberty, activities such as running, sitting, and talking may convey

Table 5.3.   Percentage of Correct Gender Attribution as Functions of the Consistency of Hair Cues with the Actual Gender of the Models, the Ages of the Models, and the Ages of the Respondents

| | Hair Cues Consistent with Model's Gender | | | | Hair Cues Inconsistent with Model's Gender | | | |
| | Model's Age | | | | Model's Age | | | |
Respondent's Age	3	8	14	18	3	8	14	18
3	48	51	55	56	48	50	50	52
8	51	53	55	58	49	51	53	55
14	60	67	83	87	55	59	62	75
18	81	85	95	100	65	78	88	95

useful gender-differentiating information. To a minimal extent, frontal views and sex-typed clothing also may be used as gender markers. But we needed a more exact estimate of the relative strengths of the various kinds of gender differentiators. The simplest and most straightforward approach was to use the same kinds of multiple and partial regression analyses that we used for the children's drawings.

These analyses yielded the results shown in Table 5.4. This table shows that the hair cues accounted for most of the variance, 74%. Adding the dynamic cue of running increased the proportion of variance accounted for to 75%, and even adding in running, sitting, and tallking (the most telling dynamic cues), the proportion rose to only 77%. The other cues did not significantly increase the power to predict gender attribution. Armed with this information, we then analyzed each of the hair cues separately. Once again, hair length contributed the heaviest weight, followed by hair style and hair color, when the contributions of the other hair variables were partialled out of the equations. The relatively low weights of the dynamic cues were not surprising, because the previous analyses showed that these cues were effective for only the older subjects judging the older models. The relatively high weights of the hair cues were surprising because even the adults showed these patterns.

Before discussing the interpretations of these results, we digress to consider gender attribution errors of the older subjects. These subjects were proficient at attributing gender, making only 8% errors, mostly for back-view figures. We wanted to know if their errors were systematic or haphazard. Did the errors occur under the same conditions or were they scattered randomly across conditions? The results showed that errors increased with the proportion of gender-ambiguous hair cues, and this relation was more pronounced for males than for females. Thus, when the models had short (male-typed) hair that had two other female-typed characteristics (both blond and curled), the most errors occurred. When short hair was combined with one other female-typed characteristic, the number of errors declined somewhat. A similar, but less pronounced pattern appeared for long (female-

Table 5.4. Regression Analysis

	Multiple R	R^2
Hair cues	.86	.74
Running	.87	.75
Sitting	.87	.76
Talking	.88	.77
Hair length	.79	.62
Hair style	.82	.68
Hair color	.86	.74

Table 5.5. Percentages of Erroneous Gender
Attributions as Functions of the Number of Ambiguous
Hair Cues

| | Number of Ambiguous Hair Cues | | | |
	0	1	2	13
Actual gender				
Female	6	10	32	40
Male	8	16	40	60

typed) hair. These relations are listed in Table 5.5. This pattern suggests that adults are influenced by constellations of hair cues, just as our preschoolers were in the first experiment reported in this chapter.

Respondents' Explanations of How They Attribute Gender

Next, we consider responses to the last query we put to each of our subjects: "How can you tell the difference between a girl and a boy?" We thought that this question would give the subjects a chance to add cues, including any idiosyncratic ones that they might find helpful. We were not sanguine about the preschooler's comments, however, because the preschoolers in the children's drawing experiment were rarely able to identify such cues. The numbers of cues mentioned increased with age, from a mean of two for preschoolers (almost invariably hair cues) to six for adults. The adults mentioned secondary sex cues the most often, including breasts, facial hair, and muscular builds. Next most often mentioned were hair length and hair style. Inferred or visible genitals were mentioned next, followed by clothing. Although adults were able to identify a number of cues they thought that they used to attribute gender, they seemed initially nonplussed by the question, a surprising reaction in view of the task they had just completed. As one person said, "I never think about it; I just look at someone and know right away what sex the person is." For the adults gender attribution has become an automatic process.

Last, we again evaluated the effects of subject's own hair characteristics and ethnic background on their correct gender attributions. These variables had no reliable or even discernible effect.

Reprise: What Are the Cues Used To Identify Gender?

This is a propitious time to summarize the outcomes of the four gender-attribution experiments. The major results from children's own drawings, pictures, and videotapes of both children and adults show a marked convergence, thereby extending their generality.

1. Hair cues are the most important gender markers for subjects from preschool to adult (all experiments). Indeed, hair cues are so important that their elimination (by covering the hair) reduces gender attribution to a chance level (two videotape experiments).

2. Running, sitting, talking, and front views are the next most important for all subjects (second videotape experiment).

3. Clothing may be used if the above cues are obscured or ambiguous (all experiments with the clearest effects in the picture and second videotape experiments).

4. Other cues, such as standing and walking are not very useful gender cues, particularly for figures in unisex clothing, viewed from the back with their hair covered (second videotape experiment).

5. The subjects appear to combine the cues, rather than relying on single ones (clearest evidence in the picture experiment).

6. Maleness is signaled by fewer, seemingly more rigid cues than those that denote femaleness (picture experiment), but

7. There is a greater tendency to guess male when the favored (hair) cues are covered. In other words, when very little information is available about a person's gender so the subjects have to guess, they are more likely to guess male than female (first videotape experiment).

8. The two sexes show identical patterns of gender attribution for both sexes of stimulus figures. Thus, we found no evidence for our subjects to be more sensitive to same-sex cues than to other-sex cues (all experiments).

9. Accurate gender attribution increases with age (drawing and two videotape experiments).

10. The same order and pattern of gender-cue effectiveness is found for different ethnic backgrounds and for subjects whose own hair characteristics deviate from the standards they are attributing to others.

11. Children not only recognize the importance of hair cues, but they also produce these cues in their own drawings of the two sexes (drawing experiment).

12. Most of our preschoolers knew their own gender; fewer understood that gender remains constant over time and still fewer, that gender remains constant over situations. Thus, the developmental acquisition of these concepts proceeds in the order of gender identity, temporal gender constancy, motivational gender constancy, and situational gender constancy. Nevertheless, this systematic progression was not related to the ability to correctly assign gender (drawing and picture experiments).

13. Most children are aware of and can reproduce at least some gender-linked given names. Once they have attributed gender, the children always stated a gender-related name if they stated one at all (picture experiment).

How robust is the apparent dependence on hair cues as gender markers? Some skepticism is warranted because these cues are imperfectly correlated with gender. Perhaps the selection of cues was so limited that the use of hair cues was artificially and spuriously elevated. This doesn't seem likely, for in the second videotape experiment, the subjects were not restricted to a limited number of hair cues; indeed, they had a substantial number of potentially relevant gender cues available to them via the facial characteristics, facial expressions, body language, and similar cues that were captured in the filming of the sequences. Even so, hair cues seemed to be particularly important at all ages. Additional support for hair cues as gender markers comes from previous research, but in those cases the various types of hair cues were not separated, nor were attempts made to compare the relative weights of different hair cues or of the hair cues versus nonhair cues. Further support stems from the observations that the same hair-gender patterns are used by subjects whose own hair does or does not depart from the norms they are imposing on the stimulus, and by minority members whose families probably have dark hair and brown eyes, regardless of their sex. These factors all suggest that the dependence on hair cues is indeed robust, at least in our society.

The most remarkable aspect of the results is the reliance on such nonpredictive cues. Of course, one could argue that, since no single cue is infallibly predictive of gender, multiple cues will be used in a combinatorial fashion. But why combine various types of hair cues? Because they are visible? Perhaps. Because these cues were learned at an early age through social learning and similar mechanisms? Perhaps. One such vehicle of social learning could be books, magazines, and similar types of reading material that introduce children to a world beyond their own experiences. Television serves the same function, of course. As noted in Chapter 4, we found no gender differences in hair characteristics in children's books, but we found television programs to be rife with such distinctions. While we cannot evaluate the impact television had on our subjects' perceptions of gender characteristics, the television data suggest a reason for the prevalence of hair characteristics as gender markers. Television is a plausible, widespread source of such information that might be incorporated into children's gender schemata (e.g., Drabman, Robertson, Patterson, Jarvie, Hammer, & Cordua, 1981; Eron, Huesman, Brice, Fischer, & Mermelstein, 1983; McGhee & Frueh, 1980; and Morgan, 1982).

The contents of these gender schemata seem to be quite varied, including gender identity, the gender constancies, and information about gender differentiators. The constituents are not necessarily interrelated; that is, they may be independent members of the gender schema, as implied by the absence of a correlation of gender attribution with the concepts of gender identity and the gender constancies.

One of the incentives for the current research was the apparent discrepancy between the cues used by children and those used by adults. These earlier findings could have been produced by testing limited sets of adult-selected cues. Our data, based on both child-referenced and extensive cues, demonstrate that children do not use genitals or secondary sex characteristics as gender markers as adults do, but children and adults both use hair and some of the dynamic activity cues. We assume that these variations reflect development of cognitive gender schemata. Other gender markers may well have escaped our attention, and we do not claim that the cues tested are the only or even the most prevalent cues used. Nonetheless, we were impressed by the large proportion of the variance accounted for by hair cues and by walking, talking, and running.

Predictions of The Theories

These data also speak to many of the predictions made by various theories and models. For example, the data deny the Freudian psychoanalytic view of genitalia as the most salient gender markers at all ages. Our young subjects yielded no such evidence. They never drew even secondary sexual characteristics, let alone genitals. Moreover, they never mentioned genitals as distinguishing features. Genital cues do not appear to be important at earlier stages of development, although they may become so from a prepubertal time onward, either in their actual physical form or as inferred gender differentiators, such as Kessler and McKenna's (1978) "cultural penis." Nor did psychonalytic variants that emphasize female-related cues at early ages receive much support. These views assume that most children, because of their early identifications with female caretakers, will be more sensitive to female-related cues than to male-related ones at least during the preschool years. Our only evidence of a bias toward one sex was in the opposite direction: In the videotaped children's study, preschool boys were more likely to guess "boy" than "girl", regardless of the gender of the stimulus person. Subsequent investigations suggested that this tendency occurred because the models had more male-related than female-related hair characteristics.

Cognitive-developmental theory proposes that the development of gender-related information will not occur until the child has achieved gender constancy. This view was refuted by our findings that children could accurately estimate the intended gender of other children's drawings before they all achieved temporal and situational constancy. Cognitive developmental theory also proposes that size will be a factor contributing to gender schemata, because children learn to associate largeness with maleness with authority. Size was immaterial in the children's drawings. Indeed, the mean height of male figures was drawn to be somewhat less than that of the female figures.

According to both the cultural genital theory and our cultural gender model, gender attribution depends on a comparison against a male-associated protocol. This is Kessler and McKenna's (1978) "cultural penis" notion. Thus, male-related cues should be preeminent. This prediction is a little harder to evaluate than the preceding ones. In explaining their model, Kessler and McKenna (1978) state that the gender decision rule is predicted on male-related attributes. If the person being judged has male-related attributes that person is called a male. If the person does not have male-related attributes, the person is a female. Our data suggest the existence of a female-related schema, in addition to the male-related one, at least at early ages. One could argue, of course, about whether or not a real (read meaningful) distinction exists between not-female/female and male/female decision rule, but a psychological distinction surely exists. The composition of the male-related protocol is far more rigidly defined than the composition of the counterpart one, and this is true from preschool to adult age.

Of the predictions from the gender schema models, the one relevant to gender attribution is that gender schemata for one's own sex will be stronger than schemata for the other gender. This prediction, derived from Martin and Halverson (1981), expects children to identify the gender of same-sex models more accurately than the gender of other-sex models. Our boys and girls were equally facile at attributing gender to same- and to other-sex stimulus persons or drawings.

The cognitive gender model assumes that children will develop gender schemata for each sex, a view that seems consistent with the data. We hasten to add, however, that this prediction also is consonant with other models, including some gender-schema versions, the social learning, cognitive-developmental, and even Freudian theories. To distinguish between these models, we need information about the similarity of children's personal or self schemata and the schemata they hold for people in general. The next experiments deal with these issues.

Reprinted by permission of News America Syndicate and Johnny Hart.

CHAPTER 6

Gender Constancy

> Girls are always girls because they can wear everything, but boys are girls only when they wear dresses.

> When I grow up I'm going to be a mommy and have a little girl. Then I'll be a daddy so I can have a little boy.

As noted in Chapters 4 and 5 and in the above quotations from three-year-old informants, not all preschoolers think that gender remains constant over time and situations. Do these results mean that young children have not yet developed the concepts of gender constancy? That interpretation is one possibility. Another possibility is that the children may be in a transition state between no awareness of gender constancy, in which their answers to gender constancy questions and their explanations of their answers are incorrect, and full awareness of gender constancy, in which their answers to gender constancy questions and the accompanying explanations are both correct. Still other possibilities are that they do not understand the questions used to assess gender constancy or that they are misled by the questions. These possibilities are quite plausible because the questions designed to probe more advanced gender constancies (e.g., temporal and situational constancies) are linguistically more complex than questions designed to index earlier gender constancies (e.g., gender identity). Consider a standard query about gender identity: "Are you a girl or a boy?" This simple question contains seven words. It does not contain any conditional clauses, embedded phrases, or other linguistic devices that might be beyond the abilities of a two-and-one-half to three-year-old child. Now consider a standard query about temporal gender constancy or stability: "When you were a little baby, were you a little boy or a little girl?" This more complex question contains 15 words and a conditional clause. It asks the young child to deal with memorial consequences of an absent event. When cast into the future, it asks the youngster to try to project to a time some 20 years hence, a formidable task for a child whose total life span at the time of questioning encompasses only about three years.

Questions about situational gender constancy also are linguistically complex, and they require the child to not only imagine a particular situation (which the child may never have experienced directly) but to guess about the intent of the questions. One standard query (in the form to be read to a girl) is, "If you played boy games, would you be a girl or a boy?" Is the experimenter asking whether the child would be pretending to be the other sex? Whether the child would really be (change into) the other sex? Either interpretation is plausible.

These concerns are troublesome, for they challenge the validity of estimates of gender constancy based on verbal questioning. We focus on these issues in Chapter 6. Resolutions of these concerns are important to our understanding of the components of gender concepts. The resolutions also are central to evaluating models of gender development, for the concepts of gender constancy and the ages of their acquisition emerge in all models of gender development; they are pivotal to Kohlberg's (1966) cognitive-developmental model. Another reason to verify knowledge of gender constancy is that we found that this knowledge is independent of the ability to correctly assign gender, a surprising, counterintuitive, highly important result that needs further exploration. These concerns, discussed in more detail below, define the domain of Chapter 6. Specifically, we set ourselves the tasks of assessing the validity of the progression of gender concepts when tested by verbal questions and perceptual tasks. Both the theoretical and empirical evidence considered so far predicts that the progression will be ordered from gender identity to temporal and motivational constancy, to situational gender constancy, with some evidence of the transitional (pseudoconstant) stage appearing before true temporal, motivational, and situational gender constancies are achieved.

Traditional Results

Accumulating evidence suggests that children learn their own gender identity (what sex they are) by about 2½ to 3 years of age (Coker, 1984; Eaton & Von Bargen, 1981; Fagot, 1985; Gouze & Nadelman, 1980; Emmerich et al., 1977; Kuhn et al., 1978; Marcus & Overton, 1978; McConaghy, 1979; Thompson, 1975; Thompson & Bentler, 1971). They then acquire the concept of temporal gender constancy, followed by "motive" or a realization that they cannot voluntarily alter their gender, and by situational gender constancy. The latter concepts apparently develop later, with situational gender constancy not always firmly established even by the second grade (Coker, 1984). Some researchers disagree with these estimates, however. For example, Fagot (1985) found that three-and-one-half-year-olds occasionally showed evidence of situational gender constancy. Indeed, all of the above studies found at least some preschoolers who showed temporal, motivational, or situational gender constancy, as we did.

Definitional Problems

Two problems which have plagued research on gender constancy are the use of different labels to name similar or identical concepts and the use of different methods to investigate the concepts. Gender identity is sometimes called labeling (Eaton & Von Bargen, 1981); temporal gender constancy has been called stability, or gender permanence, and subsumes motive (the understanding that one cannot change gender even if one wishes it to change); and situational gender constancy is often termed simply gender constancy. Gender constancy also has been classified into true and pseudoconstancy by Eaton and Von Bargen (1981), Emmerich et al. (1977), Fagot (1985) and Wehren and De Lisi (1983), with true constancy reflecting correct judgments and explanations and pseudoconstancy representing correct judgments but incorrect explanations. The pseudoconstancy explanations, which typically involve societal norms, were considered to be preoperational by Emmerich et al., (1977). We use the terms gender identity, temporal, motivational, and situational gender constancy because they seem to us to be the most descriptive. The differences in labeling could be resolved, of course, but these differences have often been allied with a more severe problem, differences in the methods and techniques used to study mastery of the various concepts.

Methodological Problems

Hence, a second, substantive difficulty is that different methods have been used to instantiate the concepts. Some research (e.g., Coker, 1984; Eaton & Von Bargen, 1981; Emmerich et al., 1977; Fagot, 1985; Marcus & Overton, 1978; Slaby & Frey, 1975; Wehren & De Lisi, 1983) has used verbal measures similar or identical to those used in the drawing experiments (Chapter 4). Other work has used a perceptual transformation task to assess situational gender constancy (Chapter 5). In the perceptual transformation task, the child is shown a model, such as a doll, putting on atypical clothing and then responds to the question, "If Janie [the doll] puts on boy clothes, what would she be, a boy or a girl?" Martin and Halverson (1983; also see Gouze & Nadelman, 1980) propose that young children may have more difficulty with perceptual transformations than with verbal measures, presumably because verbal measures do not require alterations of already perceived objects. In their experiments performance was generally higher on verbal than on the perceptual tasks, but this difference disappeared when the perceptual variants of the questions actually showed a transformation. This technique was designed to roughly equate the information conveyed by the questions. That is, in the verbal form, the child is asked whether a boy wearing a girl's clothes is a boy or a girl, whereas, in the perceptual equivalent the child sees a clothing transformation and then is asked about gender). It seems, then, that both verbal and perceptual tasks yield similar assessments of situational gender constancy when the perceptual transformation is actually shown. Nevertheless, verbal tasks have been preferred because they are easily used to estimate gender identity and the various gender constancies whereas the perceptual tasks have been used for only situational gender constancy.

The relation between gender concepts and their instantiating perceptual transformations has another potential significance. Gouze and Nadelman (1980) suggest that the perceptual change which typically accompanies transformations across situations is at least partly responsible for the slower acquisition of situational gender constancy compared to temporal and motivational constancies. The latter do not usually require perceptual transformations. This view implies that among various situations used to assess gender constancy, constancy will be acquired later for perceptual transformations, such as varying activities and appearances, than for situations that do not usually require transformations, such as personality traits. Wehren and De Lisi (1983) found no support for this prediction: Temporal gender constancy preceded situational gender constancy, but situational changes involving personality traits, activities, and appearances showed no differences. They suggest that the precedence of temporal gender constancy over situational gender constancy is more likely to result from children's developing knowledge of societal norms. Their subjects rarely used societal norms, such as the gender "appropriateness" or "inappropriateness" of activities, physical attributes, and psychological traits to "explain" temporal gender constancy (stability). In contrast, societal norms were frequently given as explanations of situational gender constancy, except when older children (seven and nine years old) stated a true understanding of gender constancy.

Martin and Halverson (1983) proposed still another explanation for the temporal-situational gender constancy order. They asserted that the children may respond on the basis of a "pretend" rather than a "real" situation. Indeed, they present evidence that suggests that gender constancy appears at younger ages when children respond to a real situation than when they respond to a pretend situation. Apparently, children have both temporal and situational gender constancy—by age three or four, according to Martin and Halverson—when they understand that the questions refer to the real world and not to a "pretend" one.

These results raise the issue of understanding the questions about gender constancy, as mentioned earlier. Gender identity questions typically refer to situations the child has experienced and presumably understands. Questions about temporal gender constancy refer to being an infant (baby) or an adult (man or woman), experiences that are alien to the child and that the child may have difficulty imagining. Questions about situational gender constancy also may probe experiences they haven't had, such as dressing in clothes usually associated with the other sex. Children may answer the temporal and situational gender constancy questions incorrectly, because they don't understand the questions.

In addition, the questions may confound the complexity of the gender concept with the linguistic complexity of the questions and the experience of the child. For example, as already noted, the question, "Are you a little girl or a little boy?"—is relatively simple. In contrast, the question, "If you wore little boy's clothes would you be a little girl or a little boy?"—is considerably more complex, raising the issue of whether or not children understand what is being asked. Simple questions are understood before complex, multiclause ones (Clark & Clark, 1977). Also linguistically complex is the question used to tap temporal gender constancy, "When you grow up will you be a man or a woman?" These experiential and linguistic differences may be responsible for apparent age differences in acquisition of the concepts about gender. Such problems are compounded by the ambiguity of the situational gender constancy questions, which could be answered in terms of what sex a person is pretending to be or what sex the person actually is and remains regardless of external transformations.

Motivated by the centrality of children's gender concepts to models of gender-role development (e.g., Kohlberg, 1966; Martin & Halverson, 1981; Mischel, 1970), we wanted to study how experiential and linguistic components affected tests of preschoolers' gender concepts. To probe the role of experience, we first determined whether or not the children had participated in various gender-typed activities. If they had participated, we then asked whether they had been girls or boys during these activities. Note that this condition assessed situational gender constancy, but not temporal gender constancy or gender identity. To minimize the use of language we presented photographs to depict gender identity, temporal gender constancy, and situational gender constancy. Last, we included standard linguistic questions to examine various kinds of gender constancy and requested children's explanations of their answers. These measures afforded comparisons with the perceptual results of the current experiment, and with our own and others' previous work, including pseudoconstancy.

Pseudoconstancy

Pseudoconstancy is a puzzle. Should it be interpreted as a preoperational intermediate stage of gender constancy, as Emmerich et al. (1977) proposed? Is it simply another reflection of the linguistic contretemps imposed on the respondents by the demands of the queries and the lack of experience of the children? Does it display a lag between children's performance and their ability to describe the performance and its origins? This lag occurs in many other areas; consequently, it may apply to gender awareness.

On the basis of a Piagetian view of developmental stages, Wehren and De Lisi (1983) predicted that true situational gender constancy would not be obtained until middle to late childhood, say about age nine. By this time, the children are expected to have progressed to the operational stage. They asked three-, five-, seven-, and nine-year-olds to answer and to explain their answers to standard gender constancy questions. The explanations were divided into three categories: no explanation, a societal norm explanation, and a constancy explanation. Most of their three-year-olds gave no explanation. A few mentioned societal norm explanations and even fewer gave a constancy explanation. The use of no explanations declined across the age groups, so that very few nine-year-olds provided no explanation. Similarly, the use of constancy explanations increased, with most nine-year-olds showing this level of sophistication. Social norm explanations increased for the five- and seven-year-olds and then declined for the nine-year-olds.

These results coincide with predictions based on a Piagetian stage model of development. They do not affirm this model (and its close cousin, Kohlberg's, 1966, cognitive developmental model), however, because no link was established between gender constancy explanations and the stage of operational development. If anything, the fairly smooth progressions across the ages of the proportions of the three types of explanations contradicts the Piagetian-Kohlbergian notion of step-like stages of development.

Unfortunately, we cannot use these or similar results to resolve the issue of the proper interpretation of pseudoconstancy, because the methodology employed in the research confounded linguistic complexity and experience with the assumed complexity of the gender concepts, as described above.

Our Experiment, Its Rationale, and Its Predictions

If the gender concepts are robust and unaffected by experiential and linguistic variables, we should find the standard sequence for preschoolers of higher awareness of gender identity, followed by lesser awareness of temporal and then of situational gender constancy. If gender concepts in previous work have been affected by experiential or linguistic differences tapped by the questions, these relationships will be altered.

The experiment contained four major conditions. The first, the verbal condition, presented the standard questions listed on the left side of Table 6.1. These are the same questions that were used in the picture experiment (Chapter 5). Four questions assessed gender identity, four questions assessed temporal gender constancy, and four more addressed situational gender constancy. These items provided us with performance of our participants

Table 6.1. Conditions and Questions Testing Gender Identity, Temporal Gender Constancy, and Situational Gender Constancy and Percentages of Correct Responses.

Verbal Condition	Photograph Condition	Experiential Condition
Gender identity 1. Are you a girl or a boy? 2. Are you a (other sex from child's first response)? 3. Does your mother call you a boy or a girl? 4. Does your mother call you a (other sex from child's first response)?	1. Picture of Susie as preschooler. Is Susie a boy or girl? 2. Picture of Johnny as preschooler. Is Johnny a girl or boy?	
Percent correct 94	96	—
Temporal gender constancy 1. When you were a little baby, were you a little boy or a little girl? 2. Were you ever a little (other sex from child's first response)? 3. When you grow up will you be a woman or a man? 4. Could you ever be a (other sex from child's first response)?	1. Picture of Johnny as a baby. Is Johnny a boy or a girl? 2. Picture of Susie as a baby. Is Susie a girl or a boy? 3. Picture of Susie as an adult. Is Susie a boy or a girl? 4. Picture of Johnny as an adult. Is Johnny a girl or a boy?	
Percent correct 80	87	—
Situational gender constancy 1. If *you* wore (other sex from child) clothes, would you be a boy or a girl? 2. If you wore (other sex from child) clothes, would you be a boy or a girl? 3. If *you* (child's name) played (other sex from child) games, would you be a girl or a boy? 4. If *you* played (other sex from child) games, would you be a (other sex from child's first response)?	1. Picture of Susie as Mandrake the Magician. Is Susie a girl or a boy? 2. Picture of Johnny as a witch. Is Johnny a boy or a girl? 3. Picture of Johnny as a teacher. Is Johnny a girl or a boy? 4. Picture of Susie as a basketball player. Is Susie a boy or a girl?	1. Have you helped your mother or someone else make cookies? If yes, "Were you a girl or a boy when you helped make the cookies?" 2. Have you helped your dad or someone else rake leaves? If yes, "Were you a boy or a girl when you helped rake leaves?"
Percent correct 63	71	91

on the standard questions used to assess the gender constancies. We needed to determine whether or not our young informers' responses mimicked those of other children.

A second, photograph, condition showed photographs designed to depict the relations tested by the questions. Thus, the photographs (see center section of Table 6.1) were selected to correspond to all of the standard verbal conditions, except for counterparts to questions 3 and 4 ("Does your mother call you a boy or a girl?" and "Does your mother call you a (opposite sex)?"). For the girl sequence, the photographs showed a preschooler, a baby, a young adult, a young teenager receiving a trophy for playing basketball, and the same teenager dressed as Mandrake the Magician for Halloween. The boy sequence was similar, showing a preschooler, a baby, a young adult, a young teenager "playing teacher" by reading to some younger children, and the same teenager dressed like a witch for Halloween. In each case, the experimenter stressed that the photographs in each series portrayed the same person at different ages. The photograph condition should graphically represent each gender concept, thereby minimizing confusions which might have been present in the verbal condition.

The "own experience" condition contained the questions shown on the right side of Table 6.1. These questions were designed to test the child's comprehension of situational gender constancy when the child herself or himself had participated in the described experiences.

Finally, to estimate the extent to which the children thought the two sexes participated in activities mentioned in the various probes of situational gender constancy, they were asked to indicate whether girls or boys usually engaged in the situations listed in Table 6.2. These situations were exemplars of dressing in gender-typed clothes (wearing an apron or overalls; dressing up as a witch or as Mandrake the Magician on Halloween) or participating in gender-typed activities (baking cookies, raking leaves, pretending to be a teacher, receiving a trophy for prowess as a basketball player). In all cases, children were asked to explain their answers.

We gave the battery to 175 subjects (60 girls and 115 boys). These children, aged 3.1 to 4.5 years, attended local preschools. Approximately 70% were white, 15% were Black, 10% were Hispanic, and 5% were Asian American. The children were mostly upper middle class. Approximately half of the girls and half of the boys were tested by two female experimenters and the other subjects were tested by male experimenters.

Half of the children served in the verbal condition before the photograph condition. The other half served in the opposite order. The "own" experience test and the test for gender assignment always were presented as the third and fourth tests.

The results are divided into two major sections. The first focuses on the experiential tests. The second considers the results from the standard verbal questions and from the photograph conditions. Neither the sex of the respondent nor the sex of the experimenter qualified any of the following conclusions. This means that the boys and girls answered in similar ways, regardless of the sex of the experimenter. Consequently, the sex of the respondent and of the experimenter will not be discussed further.

Gender Constancy for Experienced Conditions

When the children had engaged in the described activity and therefore qualified for the questions about their gender while participating in the activity, 91% answered the situational gender constancy questions correctly. This performance was significantly higher than that for comparable situational gender constancy tests in the linguistic (63%) and photographic (71%) conditions, $F(2, 348) = 14.31$, $p < .001$. This analysis was based on the number of situational gender constancy questions answered correctly as a function of the three conditions (actually had participated, linguistic, and photographic). Clearly, when the children had experienced the situation, most of them were aware that their own gender had not changed. Moreover, their performance on these purportedly difficult situational gender questions did not differ reliably from the percentages on the supposedly easy gender identity questions when tested by the linguistic condition (94%) or the photograph condition (96%), $F(2, 348) = 1.93$, $p < .05$. We were astonished by these results, for they suggested that most of our 3- and 4-year-olds could correctly answer questions about situational gender constancy, an outcome not reported by any of the earlier studies.

Before drawing firm conclusions, we need to consider the frequency with which the children had participated in the tested activities. If only a few children had participated, the results would not be generalizable. This was not the case. The range in participation in the activities was from 80% (wearing an apron) to 100% (baking cookies, raking leaves). Thus, the results of the experiential test were generally representative of the children. The other potential qualification of the results was that our subjects might not consider the activities of the experiential test as gender-typed. As their last task, all subjects were asked whether girls or boys usually engaged in each of the activities. As shown in Table 6.2, our subjects showed the expected gender typing. Most of the children stated that girls make cookies, wear aprons, are teachers, and dress up like witches on Halloween, whereas boys rake leaves, wear overalls, are basketball players, and dress up like Mandrake the Magician on Halloween. Thus, their generally high level of performance on the situational gender constancy questions in the experiential condition cannot be attributed to the absence of gender typing of the test's activities and situations. Instead, our results appear to reflect the

Table 6.2.   Percentages of Respondents Claiming that Females or Males Usually Engage in the Stated Activities.

Who usually...	Percentages	
	Girls	Boys
1. dresses up like a witch at Halloween?	76	24
2. dresses up like Mandrake the Magician at Halloween?	27	73
3. pretends to be a teacher?	68	32
4. wins trophies for being a star basketball player?	21	79
5. makes cookies?	76	24
6. wears overalls?	33	67
7. wears an apron?	75	25
8. rakes leaves?	24	76

more sensitive approach of probing experiences with which they had some familiarity. In this situation, they knew that their sex had not changed, and they were able to correctly answer the questions about situational gender constancy.

But did they really understand the concept of situational gender constancy? Were they able to explain their answers on the basis of true constancy over situations? Following the general scoring procedure reported in Chapters 4 and 5 which we had adapted from Wehren and De Lisi (1983), we asked one experimenter and one person who was naive to all of our experimentation to assign the explanations to the three categories of no explanation, an explanation based on societal norms, and an explanation based on constancy. The two differed on the assignment of only one explanation, which was resolved by discussion.

The 175 respondents each answered two experientially related situational gender constancy questions. Of the 319 correct answers given to the situational gender constancy questions, 110 or 35% gave constancy explanations. These results stand in marked contrast to the 1% for three-year-olds and 2% for five-year-olds found by Wehren and De Lisi (1983) for questions relating to the self. As shown in Table 6.3, the other explanations were divided almost equally between no explanation (103) and social norm explanations (106). These differences seem to be the result of using gender-related activities with which the child was familiar, rather than referring to vaguely specified, and probably nonexperienced activities.

Gender Constancy for Verbal and Photographic Conditions

As expected from previous work (e.g., Coker, 1984; Eaton & Von Bargen, 1981; Emmerich et al., 1977; Marcus & Overton, 1978; Slaby & Frey, 1975; Thompson, 1975; Thompson & Bentler, 1971) the verbal questions yielded a

Table 6.3.   Percentages of Explanations Falling into Three Explanatory Categories. The Explanations Followed Correct Responses to Gender Constancy Questions.

		Condition	
	Verbal	Photograph	Experiential
Temporal gender constancy			
No explanation	40	41	—
Social explanation	45	37	—
Constancy explanation	15	22	—
Situational gender constancy			
No explanation	51	45	32
Social explanation	41	42	33
Constancy explanation	8	13	35

Note: All entries were based on four gender constancy conditions except for the entries for experiential situational gender constancy, which were based on two questions. The number of respondents was 175.

decline in the percentages of questions answered correctly from 94% for gender identity to 80% for temporal gender constancy to 63% for situational gender constancy. Representations of the same situations by photographs showed superior overall performance (the mean percentages of correct responses for the verbal and the photograph conditions were 79 and 85, respectively, $F(1, 174) = 4.13$, $p < .05$). The photograph condition also showed a decrease in proficiency over the three gender concepts, but the trend was less marked: gender identity (96%), temporal gender constancy (87%), and situational gender constancy (71%). An analysis of variance corroborated the decline over the gender concepts, $F(2, 348) = 34.77$, $p < .001$. The interaction between the three gender concepts and their presentation in linguistic and photographic settings was not reliable, however, $F < 1$. The percentages for the three concepts each differed reliably from the others and from a chance-level performance. Thus, assessing the gender concepts by descriptive photographs yielded the same patterning of gender concepts as the verbal questions which varied in linguistic complexity, but the photographs elicited greater awareness of the various gender constancies. Although we cannot target linguistic complexity as a culprit that has suppressed evidence of gender constancy competence, our findings testify to the greater sensitivity of perceptual tests of gender constancy. We see no reason to continue to use tasks that vary in their linguistic demands when these demands are irrelevant to the issue in question.

The difference in the sensitivity between the perceptual and linguistic tasks was further illuminated by the explanations. Once again, the same two individuals assigned explanations to the three explanation categories. This exercise was carried out for correctly answered temporal and situational gender constancy questions as functions of the condition (verbal and photograph). They agreed on all but three explanations, and the disposition of these items was decided by discussion. For temporal gender constancy, constancy explanations were given for 15% of the verbal condition questions and for 22% of the photograph conditions. No explanations were given for about 40% of the questions in these conditions (Table 6.3). For situational gender constancy, the most obvious differences were the higher percentages of constancy explanations for the photograph than for the verbal condition, and the declines in the numbers of constancy explanations from those given for temporal gender constancy questions and from the experiential condition for situation gender constancy.

How do we explain these findings? We couldn't have inadvertently sampled a group of particularly gender sophisticated children, because their performance was not stellar when they responded to the verbal questions. The results couldn't be due to order effects, because of the counterbalancing. We conclude that they are due to the original manipulations—that children really do possess substantial knowledge about gender stability and constancy. Their knowledge can be demonstrated by using simple tasks that are related to events and activities that are familiar to them. Finally, we analyzed separately the question about motivation (Temporal gender constancy question no. 4). The results indicated that motivational gender constancy was about the same as the other questions about temporal gender constancy in terms of the frequency of correct answers and explanations.

How does this performance compare with that found by other researchers? In addition to the Wehren-De Lisi (1983) results already discussed, we can examine a few others, although exact comparisons are difficult because the ages of the subjects have varied from experiment to experiment. Nevertheless, the percentages of children exhibiting situational gender constancy ranged from 16% of Emmerich et al.'s (1977) children with a mean age of 69 months (tested with a perceptual transformation task) to 95% of Martin and Halverson's (1983) children with a mean age of 67 months, an amazing range. Martin and Halverson's estimate was based on verbal questions when the children were asked to respond "for real." Apparently, our use of situations actually experienced by the children achieves much the same effect as asking them to respond "for real."

Summing Up

In brief, when preschoolers with a mean age of 45 months have experienced situations themselves, 91% of them manifested substantial knowledge of situational gender constancy, knowledge that may have been underestimated by previous research that tested situations of unknown familiarity.

Our results imply that to the limited extent that children's concepts of situational gender constancy are deficient, the deficiency stems from difficulties in comprehending the linguistic meaning of the questions, to extrapolating to unknown situations, or to other people. This outcome supports the contention that children develop knowledge about their own gender before extrapolating this knowledge to others (Eaton & Von Bargen, 1981; Gouze & Nadelman, 1980; Marcus & Overton, 1978; Wehren & De Lisi, 1983). Our results indicate further that children are no more sensitive to same-sex than to other-sex cues, as also found in our previous work and by others (e.g., Wehren & De Lisi, 1983), but not by Eaton and Von Bargen (1981). Although Eaton and Von Bargen's finding of same-sex before other-sex sensitivity is at odds with most other results, their more substantial observation that self-cues preceded awareness of other cues corresponded to standard demonstrations.

Our subjects' proficiency with gender constancy is not as effectively assessed by photographic portrayal or by only verbal questions as by the experiential condition. Indeed, standard verbal questions appear to be a relatively insensitive measure of these concepts. We were surprised that the photographic depiction of situational gender constancy, in particular, did not improve performance as much as the experiential condition. These findings now are explained by the experiential results, for the photographs simply did not test familiar individuals. Youngsters apparently understand gender constancies as these concepts refer to themselves before they attribute the constancies to other people.

What are the implications for models of gender development (e.g., Kohlberg, 1966; Martin & Halverson, 1981; Mischel, 1970)? Clearly, children possess more information about concepts of gender constancy than previously thought. They apparently acquire knowledge about the identity and constancy of their own gender during their first three years, but they are not necessarily able to generalize these concepts to unknown situations or to others. In later childhood, they acquire the ability to generalize gender concepts to others and to nonexperienced situations. These views are similar to those advanced by Eaton and Von Bargen (1981), Gouze and Nadelman (1980), Marcus and Overton (1978), and Wehren and De Lisi (1983), among others. We suggest further, that, during later development, the components of the gender concepts may be further elaborated. That is, rather than establishing new types of concepts about the operation of one's own and others' gender, the concepts acquired in very early childhood become increasingly complex and diversified through elaboration as the child's range of experiences increases. Overall, the data vividly demonstrate that young children have more complex and sophisticated gender constancy concepts than the models or previous, more limited research, had suggested.

BREAK IT TO HER GENTLY, RUFFLES AND LACE ARE NOT
THE REAL ME.

CHAPTER 7

Components of Children's Gender Concepts

We now know that children rely more on various hair cues to identify gender than on other cues and that their awareness of their own gender identity develops during the child's first few years, along with some knowledge of the kinds of toys, playmate preferences, and occupations typically associated with each sex. When tested with situations they themselves have experienced, preschoolers show temporal gender constancy, and then situational gender constancy. The ability to generalize the constancies to other persons and to unfamiliar situations comes later. Presumably, these concepts are part of their gender concepts. But what about other aspects of gender concepts? Do children associate particular personality traits with girls and boys or with women and men? For example, do they think that most girls are considerate, active, understanding, and athletic? Do they think that boys have the same characteristics? What about adults? Do young children attribute the same traits to women that they do to girls? Do they assign similar traits to men and boys? In brief, we wanted to identify important constituents of children's gender concepts and to see how these constituents changed with age (also see Deaux, 1982; Major, Carnevale, & Deaux, 1981).

All of the models of gender-role development assume that children's gender concepts change with age and experience, although the models detail neither the precise nature of the changes nor the ages (or stages) at which each will occur. The central notion is that the *constituents* of gender concepts change with age. If this is true, we would expect to find some differences in the gender concepts that children hold for most children and those they hold for most adults, and these differences should change with the age of the children. These changes may take different forms. New constituents may be added, some may be deleted, and others may change in importance as the person matures. Indeed, some recent work (Carter & Patterson, 1982; Garrett, Ein, & Tremaine, 1977; Tremaine, Schau, & Busch, 1982) suggests that older children (fifth to eighth graders) are more flexible in gender-typing than younger children (kindergartners, first graders). The older children were more likely than the younger ones to assume that both sexes could participate in various adult occupations. Carter and Patterson (1982) showed similar effects for children's toys. Do these results mean that toys and adult occupations drop out of the gender concepts somewhere between grades 1 and 5? Or were the originally atypical associations being added to the gender concepts, so that, for example, the possibility of girls playing with cars and of boys playing with dolls increased with age, while the possibilities of typical associations (e.g., girls playing with dolls and boys with cars) were maintained?

Carter and Patterson's results support the latter view. They found that 85% of the kindergartners stereotypically assigned the toys, a percentage that increased to 94 for sixth graders. The parallel percentages for adult occupations were 75 and 86. Obviously, the children recognized stereotypic views. Even so, with age, they became increasingly aware that neither gender exclusively dominates these areas. As the children mature, they realize that both genders may play with various kinds of toys and participate in various occupations. Lohaus and Trautner (in press) reported similar results.

Our next project pursues these issues for activities, physical, and personality characteristics, in addition to occupations. In general terms, we compare the constituents of children's gender concepts for most children with those for most adults, using preschool and older children as our subjects.

Our first experimental problem was to identify the constituents to be tested. Certain cues are obvious possibilities, such as physical characteristics, activities, apparel, and personality traits. At some ages, children may distinguish between the sexes on the basis of physical cues like eye color, size, genitals, hair cues, body contours, physical strength, and musculature. They may use clothing (e.g., boys wear pants or shorts all of the time; girls wear dresses plus pants and shorts) or activities (e.g., women are in service roles, often in the home, such as cooking, cleaning, caring for others; men are in more instrumental roles, often outside the home, such as directing others, making business transactions, operating equipment; girls play with dolls and skip rope; boys play with trucks and shoot baskets). Children may differentiate on the basis of personality traits, such as niceness, independence, competitiveness, and warmth.

Previous work gives us some insight into what children either think about themselves or what they think about men and women. Even three-year-olds have gender-typed preferences for toys, activities, and playmates (Thompson, 1975). Moreover, young children obviously have incorporated some knowledge about adult activities into their gender concepts, for five- to

eight-year olds easily separate tools used by adults into gender-typed classifications (Nadelman, 1974), and five-year-olds classify adult occupations in
terms of the sex predominating in the occupation (Carter & Patterson, 1982;
Garrett, Ein, & Tremaine, 1977; Tremaine & Schau, 1979; Tremaine et al.,
1982). School-age children also tend to gender-type certain personality
traits. For example, Best, Williams, and Briggs (1980), Wehren and De Lisi
(1983), and Williams et al., (1975) report that children as young as five years
assign traits such as aggressiveness, independence, and self confidence to
men and gentleness, emotionality, and dreaminess, to women. These patterns also emerge cross-culturally (Best et al., 1977; Carlsson, Andersson,
Berg, & Jaderquist, 1980; Lohaus & Trautner (in press); Tarrier & Gomes,
1981; Trautner, Sahm, & Steverman, 1983; and Williams & Best, 1982).

When would we expect these components to become part of gender concepts? Two models make predictions. The first (e.g., Gouze & Nadelman,
1980; Wehren & De Lisi, 1983) is based on the notion that gender constancies
that do not involve perceptual variations will be acquired before those that
do. In other words, it is easier for the child to learn that certain personality
traits are associated with each sex than to learn that gender is constant over
situations. With personality traits, no perceptual transformation is required.
Hence this is an easier task than one that requires perceptual transformation
(e.g., imagining a change from one set of clothes to another set more often
worn by the other sex) plus learning to associate some attribute with one of
the other sex. On this model, gender associations about personality characteristics should precede those about activities, occupations, and physical
appearance.

The second model, the one that we have espoused, posits that the more
obvious, salient, and discriminable the cues distinguishing the two sexes, the
earlier these cues will be incorporated into gender concepts. The rationale is
obvious. As Perry and Bussey (1979) stated,

> Children discern behaviors appropriate to the two sexes by observing differ-
> ences between the sexes in the frequency with which they perform various re-
> sponses in a given situation and, furthermore. . . children use these abstractions
> concerning sex-appropriate behaviors as guides to their own performance in
> similar situations. (p. 1708)

The emphasis here is on observation. What is apparent, obvious, detecta-
ble, "seeable," will attract attention and is therefore available for encoding,
for learning. What is hidden, internal, obscured, "unseeable," will attract
less attention, if any at all. And it is almost a truism in cognitive psychology
that what is not attended is less likely to be encoded or learned. It follows
that information, including gender-referenced input, is more likely to be
garnered about clear patterns of movements like activities, including occu-

pations, and physical appearance than about internalized characteristics such as independence, integrity, and honesty. Personality differences between the sexes tend to be far more subtle than the other possible differentiating variables. Thus, this model predicts that activities, occupations, and physical appearance will be learned before personality traits. Although this approach seems to us to be a reasonable and defensible one, we must note that Wehren and De Lisi (1983) found no differences in the order of acquisition of these types of traits for three-, five-, seven-, and nine-year-olds.

The piecemeal evidence cited above, culled from many different sources, does not provide a systematic testing of the constituents of gender concepts that children hold for children and for adults, nor does it detail changes in gender concepts for younger and older groups of children. To further complicate matters, while some of these results cited above have received substantial support, others are controversial. For example, Best et al. (1977) and Williams et al. (1975) report that male stereotypes are learned earlier than female stereotypes, but neither Carlsson et al. (1980), in their study of Swedish children's gender-role concepts, nor Trautner, Sahm, & Steverman (1983), working with German children, replicated this result. The difference may reflect cultural differences, unreliability of the phenomenon, or limitations of the designs. Limitations of design are particularly troublesome, because they challenge the basic findings. A major problem with much of the cited research on gender-typing of personality traits is that it used a particular technique, the forced-choice approach, which may have imposed potentially biasing constraints on the results (also see Trautner et al., 1983).

The forced-choice technique requires the subjects to assign a trait to females or to males. The child is not offered the choices of saying both sexes, neither sex, or the extent to which both sexes manifest the trait. For example, in the typical situation, a child hears a brief description of a behavior and must then decide whether the actor was a female or a male. The procedure forces the child to select one sex and, in effect, to reject the other. This outcome would be acceptable if the child thought that the chosen sex always manifested the behavior and that the other sex never did—but it is not acceptable in other situations. Suppose the child thinks that both sexes might show the behavior, and yet the child must choose. The child might think that most men (say 90%) and very few women (perhaps 20%) possess it. Let us suppose further that the child judges that 60% of men and 55% of women possess another trait. In both cases the child makes a choice in accord with the higher percentage, although the situations are markedly different. Correspondingly, the procedure is not satisfactory if the child thinks that both sexes *rarely* display the behavior. The child's choice in this situation would not distinguish between differences of, say, 6% females versus 4% males and 100% females versus 0% males.

To repeat, a vexing problem with the forced-choice procedure is that it does not allow participants to indicate how often they think the traits are associated with each sex, with the result that the forced choice procedure inevitably inflates evidence for gender stereotyping. When no option for saying "same," or its equivalent (such as assigning equal probabilities of incidence for the two sexes) is available, the person must make a choice that affirms the trait for one sex and rejects it for the other.

The forced choice procedure also may constrain the classifications the child considers possible: Once children have chosen one sex, they may find it difficult to imagine that the other sex could engage in the behavior. The first choice may set up "conceptual blinders." This effect occurs in other kinds of research. For example, if children use one categorization scheme, say color, when sorting items classifiable in terms of both color and size, they are highly resistant to using any other classifications (e.g., Medin, 1973). They balk at employing even obvious alternative categories (Cunningham & Odom, 1978; Smith, 1983). Consequently, for children, any approach that begins with a forced-choice task incurs the risk of establishing biases against alternative sorting schemes.

At this point, we pause to consider the rationale for using the forced-choice technique. It avoids (a) indecision (and children are notoriously indecisive) and (b) a "yea-saying" bias (Williams & Morland, 1976) of simply agreeing with everything asked of them. The forced-choice technique appears to reduce this bias by presenting two clear alternatives to them. These positive attributes are important, and we tried to incorporate their virtues into our design while also giving children more latitude in their responses.

In sum, the forced-choice procedure may overestimate evidence for gender-stereotyping. One purpose of this research is to assess children's concepts of adults' gender-typed behaviors in a nonforced-choice paradigm, as well as in the standard forced-choice approach. The standard forced-choice paradigm is included for purposes of comparison, of course. It would be useful to know how much forced choice influences the evidence of gender stereotyping.

A second purpose is to assess children's concepts of children's gender roles. Because most of the research to date has assumed that children model their own behavior after adult sex roles, the experimental spotlight has been on children's views of adult sex roles. A few studies, however, have examined children's gender-trait ascriptions to other children. For example, Davis, Williams, and Best (1982) tested third graders for both self and peer descriptions, and Haugh, Hoffman, and Cowan (1980) probed the traits that preschoolers ascribed to infants. In general, this work, typically based on a forced-choice technique, found standard evidence of gender-typing, but, because no comparable assignments to adults were tested, adult and child gender-typing cannot be directly compared. Such comparisons are essential to understanding the development of gender schemata.

A third purpose was to developmentally track gender-typing with materials that have been standardized for both adults and children (as is true of the adjective-check list items used by Williams, Best, and their associates). We also wanted to test physical characteristics, activities, and occupations, in addition to personality traits, so we sought a format that would accommodate all of these items. The children's version of the Personal Attributes Questionnaire (Hall & Halberstadt, 1980), and the adult scale from which it was derived, Spence and Helmreich's (1978) Personal Attributes Questionnaire, seemed ideal for our use. This instrument quantifies trait assignments to each sex. The final purpose was to compare the attributes children ascribe to others to those they assign to themselves.

We selected 16 traits from the children's version of the Personal Attributes Questionnaire (Hall & Halberstadt, 1980). Eight of the traits (aware of feelings of others, considerate, emotional, gentle, kind, likes children, understanding, and warm) were of the "expressive-communal" type often associated with females, and eight (active, acts as a leader, athletic, competitive, decisive, feels superior, independent, and self-confident) were of the "instrumental-agentic" nature often associated with males (Spence & Helmreich, 1978). Brief stories or vignettes were written to translate each of the traits into behavior that could be understood by children (see Table 7.1). These stories were ecologically valid, and the children seemed to enjoy them. These stories were pretested in two ways. First, 10 female and 10 male preschoolers in a pilot study were asked to "tell what the story meant." The children had no difficulty responding to this task, suggesting that they understood the concepts. Second, 30 male and 30 female college students were asked to indicate whether the story described typical females or typical males. They also were asked to state the adjective that first came to mind as they read the story. On both counts, the stories corresponded to standard adult gender stereotypes of the intended adjectives.

After the stories had been chosen following the pretesting, adult versions were written, as well, so that we would be able to assess gender-role assignments to children or adults.

After each story (behavioral description) had been read the experimenters (one female and one male) asked the questions indicated by the forced- or nonforced-choice conditions. For the forced-choice condition the child had to decide which sex displayed the target behavior. Thus, after the behavioral description, the child was asked, "Would girls or boys do _____?" The critical portion of the story would be repeated. Next, to assess whether this choice constrained the child to deny that the other sex could manifest the behavior, or whether the child thought the other sex could partake, the respondent was asked, "Would a (other sex from that of the first response) do _____?" Two more questions tested possible extension to most members of the sexes. Thus, this approach enabled us to ascertain whether the child thought each sex could display the behavior and if so, if most members of the sex would show the behavior. These questions were, "Would most girls do that?" and "Would most boys do that?" Half of the first and third ques-

Table 7.1.   Expressive and Instrumental Adjectives and the Questions about the Behavioral Correlates in the Stories.

Adult Adjective(s)	Behavioral Correlates
Expressive traits (F)	
Aware of feelings of others	"I almost always notice how other people are feeling.
Considerate	"I am a considerate person."
Emotional	"I can never hide my emotions."
Gentle	"Yes, I guess I am a gentle person."
Kind	"I like to be kind to other people."
Likes children	"I like younger kids and babies a lot."
Understanding	"...it is easy for me to understand what other people are feeling."
Warm	"Are you friendly to other people, too?" "Oh, yes."
Instrumental traits (M)	
Active	"You're right, I am busier and more active than most..."
Acts as a leader	"...follow me! I am often the leader among my friends."
Athletic	"I guess I am pretty good at sports."
Competition	"I hate to lose a game or have other kids do better."
Decisive	"I know I have made up my mind."
Feels superior	"In most ways, I am better than most of the other _____ my age."
Independent	"I would rather do things for myself than ask...for help."
Self-confident	"Most of the time, I am sure that I am right."

Other Attributes

Female-related	Male-related
Physical attributes	
Long hair	Brown eyes
Curly hair	Dark hair
Little	Strong
Activities	
Sews	Stands while urinating
Gets dressed up	Plays baseball
Cooks	Takes out garbage
Occupations	
Nurse	Doctor
Secretary	Truck driver
Babysitter	Police officer

tions in each set referred to females first, and half, to males first. The fourth question always named the sex opposite to the one cited first in the first question of the set. The questions for the adult versions referred to women and men.

The nonforced-choice format was designed to avoid making the subjects choose between the two sexes. Thus, these questions used the following forms: "Would a girl do _____?" "Would a boy do _____?" "Would most girls do _____?'' and ''Would most boys do _____?'' As with the forced-choice question sets, half of these questions began with one sex, and half with the other. The adult versions referred to men and women.

The stories also described the physical attributes, activities, and occupations listed in Table 7.1. We chose one of the activity questions, ''Stands when peeing,'' to probe whether subjects would make the gender-genital association of males, but not females, standing while urinating. The questions following these attributes were the same as those used following the behavioral correlates of personality traits. The stories were randomly ordered and printed out for each subject. Last, we asked the children to say if each description told how *they themselves* ''really are.''

Three groups of subjects were used: preschoolers, fourth graders, and eighth graders. Forty girls and 40 boys were tested at each age level. The mean ages of the three groups were four years, one month; nine years, four months; and 13 years, six months. Minority children constituted about 20% of each of the age-sex groupings. All of the children were considered middle-class by their teachers.

Scoring Gender-"Traditional" and Gender-"Nontraditional" Responses

To make our data tractable, we computed four gender-''traditional'' and four gender-''nontraditional'' scores for each subject. For the gender-traditional scores, we assigned one point for each trait attributed to the sex with which it has been culturally associated. For example, one point was scored for each female-related trait assigned to most girls. The sum of these points was the subject's gender-traditional score for most female children. The same procedure was used to compute gender-traditional scores for the female-related traits assigned to most women. For male stimulus persons, these scores represented the total number of male-related traits that had been assigned to most boys or to most men. The next step in the scoring procedure was to calculate four gender-nontraditional scores for each subject (i.e., one score was the sum of the number of female-related traits that were assigned to most boys, and so on). These scores represented the total number of traits stereotypically assigned to one sex that our subjects attributed to the other sex stimulus person. The maximum score for each category, per person, was 17 (eight personality traits, three physical traits, three activities, and three occupations, as defined in Table 7.1).

With this scoring procedure we could easily define both gender *typing* and gender *stereotyping.* Gender *typing,* the reliable attribution of certain characteristics to a sex, regardless of cultural norms (gender traditionality or gender nontraditionality), would be indexed by scores that exceeded a chance level of assignment. Note that both male and female stimulus persons could be gender-typed for both male- and female-associated items. Gender-*stereotyping* would appear as reliable *differences* between the mean gender-traditional and gender-nontraditional scores for each sex. For example, female-stereotyped schemata would be defined as assigning female-related traits to females (gender-traditional scores) but not to males (gender-nontraditional scores). For male-stereotyped schemata, male-related traits would be assigned to males (gender-traditional scores) but not to females (gender-nontraditional scores). Two other combinations of trait assignments are conceptually possible, but pragmatically unlikely (assigning female-related traits to males but not to females and assigning male-related traits to females but not to males). These combinations rarely appeared. The combinations of assigning both or neither female- and male-related traits to each sex appear as gender-typing.

One might protest our definition of gender typing on the grounds that if both sexes are accorded the traits, these traits do not differentiate between the sexes and may not contribute to gender concepts at all. Indeed, they may be part of a "people" (sex unspecified) concept. It is true that we may be dealing with a "people" concept, but it is also true that, by the gender-typing definition, these traits must be affirmed for both sexes above a chance level. Remember, the nonforced-choice procedure allows the subject to reject the traits for one or both sexes. Moreover, the stringent above-chance requirement should reduce the likelihood of calling traits gender-typed when in fact their assignments reflect a yea-saying bias (Williams & Morland, 1976).

Our first concern is whether the subjects gender-type, as would be expected if they have gender concepts. If they do have gender concepts and if their concepts contain the gender-related items we tested, the respondents' assignments should reflect these gender associations. As an example, the respondents might believe that most males are independent and that most females are considerate, just as they also think that most females are independent and most males are considerate. If these assignments exceed chance, we consider them to be gender-typed. If the assignments are systematically associated with one but not the other sex, we consider them to be gender-stereotyped. This distinction is important, of course, because the nonforced-choice technique, but not the forced-choice procedure, gives subjects the latitude of assigning the traits to one, both, or neither of the sexes. The nonforced-choice technique should give us a firm basis for identifying gender-stereotypic traits that are expressly affirmed for one sex while being expressly rejected for the other, a comparison that is excluded by the forced-choice procedure. To examine the evidence of gender typing and gender stereotyping in gender concepts, we begin with the results from the nonforced procedure, and then consider the results from the forced-choice task.

Gender-typing and Gender-stereotyping:
Evidence from Nonforced-Choices

The nonforced-choice data tell us that, for the traits as a whole, fourth and eighth graders gender-type, but preschoolers do not. Thus, fourth and eighth graders reliably assign gender-related traits to both sexes, whereas preschoolers assign the traits at an overall level that is close to chance. Indeed, the mean number of gender assignments increased with the age of the respondent, $F(2, 234) = 460.18$, $p < .001$. As people age from three to at least nine, they attribute increasing numbers of characteristics to each of the sexes. This pattern can be seen in both the left and the right panels of Figure 7.1. The mean gender *typing* assignments of traits increased from age three to age nine and then remained constant to age 13. This can be seen most easily by imagining where the mean of the points plotted for age 13 would fall. For both panels, it would be almost "due east" of the mean gender typing scores for age nine. The absence of an increase into the teens is interesting, for it is consistent with earlier work that indicates a growth in gender typing into middle childhood with little increase thereafter (but accompanied by changes such as those we will see in gender *stereotyping*).

The age of the stimulus person also was important. Adult stimulus persons were gender typed more than young stimulus persons, $F(1, 234) = 45.04$, $p < .001$. Again, Figure 7.1 displays this difference clearly. Our youthful observers seem to be telling us that, in their eyes, adults are more gender-typed than children. Most interesting is the statistically significant interaction between these two variables, $F(2, 234) = 52.68$, $p < .001$. As Figure 7.1 displays graphically, the gender typing of adults increases more with age of the respondents than does the gender typing of children. Succinctly stated, fourth and eighth graders gender type adults more than they gender type children. Their gender concepts, then, apparently contain age information. Women and men have more gender-related traits than girls and boys have. The gender concepts of preschoolers are not as differentiated.

Fourth and eighth graders may gender-type, but do they gender-stereotype? Do they, or do preschoolers, differentially attribute traits to one sex or the other? Remember, the distinction between gender-typing and gender-stereotyping is that with gender-stereotyping, traits are attributed *significantly more often* to one than to the other sex.

Figure 7.1 conveys a number of messages. On the one hand, preschoolers do not gender-stereotype. The situation becomes somewhat more complex with older respondents. Fourth graders do not differentially assign stereotypic male traits more often to males (either boys or men) than to females (either girls or women). They do attribute reliably more stereotypically female traits to adult women than to adult men, but no difference emerges

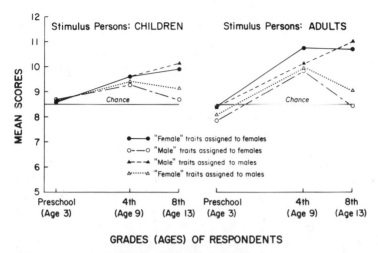

Figure 7.1   Mean gender-typing scores for four stimulus groups (girls, boys, women, men) by preschoolers, fourth- and eight-graders, nonforced choice.

among their attributions to children, implying that, if anything, attributes about females enter the gender concepts earlier than those about males. Scientific prudence, however, cautions us to reserve judgment about this issue until the rest of the data have been considered.

Figure 7.1 suggests that the eighth graders do gender-stereotype, for they assign female-related traits more often to females than to males and male-related traits more often to males than to females. Do they gender-stereotype one sex more than the other? The clearest evidence comes from the solid circles and triangles in Figure 7.1. Although these plots suggest that males might be gender-stereotyped somewhat more than females, the differences are not statistically significant. Moreover, the differences themselves are quite small. Now consider the open circles and triangles. Here we find some interesting, and unexpected differences. Eighth graders were *less* likely to attribute male traits to females than female traits to males. It is almost as though they wanted girls and women to have only female traits, but they were willing to include a few female traits along with the male traits in their attributions to males. Figure 7.1 also tells us that, eighth graders gender-stereotyped more of their attributions to adults than to children. So far, the results indicate that, in terms of gender stereotyping, the data show increasing evidence of differentiation of the sexes through age 13, the highest age tested.

These data, then, tell an interesting story about gender concept development. At least with our materials, preschoolers do not associate either female- or male-related traits with each sex above a chance level. Their gender concepts seem to be relatively impoverished compared to those of the older subjects. In contrast, fourth graders' gender concepts seem to have many components that apply to both genders. When given the opportunity to assign traits to both sexes, they systematically and significantly assign instrumental traits to both males and females, just as they assign expressive traits to both sexes. Only the eighth graders showed systematic evidence of gender-stereotyping, and they gender-stereotyped adults to an even greater degree than children.

Should we conclude that our preschoolers did not have gender concepts, whereas the older children did have them? Should we conclude that the constituents of fourth graders' female and male concepts are similar? Both conclusions would be premature, for the above analyses, based on total scores, do not divulge information about the assignments of individual items. Some items may be gender-differentiators, whereas others are not—at any of the ages we tested. Other items may be differentiators at some but not at all of the tested ages. For example, physical attributes, activities, and occupations ostensibly function as gender differentiators by age three (Thompson, 1975; Tremaine & Schau, 1979). Personality traits, which are more subtle, elusive, difficult to detect, may take longer to develop than other types of cues. These traits may not become functional until later. Accordingly, we considered the gender typing of each item by tallying the percentage of students classifying each item in gender-traditional or nontraditional ways.

All ages of subjects, including the preschoolers, claimed that both girls and woman are little with curly, long hair. Women sew and cook. Nurses, secretaries, and babysitters are women. Fourth and eighth graders have added "likes children," and "warm" to the list of female attributes. Eighth graders also include "being understanding." These data also contained a surprise for us, although our earlier work with gender attribution should have prepared us for it: Preschoolers thought females were almost as likely as men to stand while urinating. Quite a few fourth graders shared this belief, but only a few eighth graders did. To summarize the overall results, the collection of female traits shows the expected development of physical traits, activities, and occupations before the personality traits.

A similar pattern emerged for the male traits. In this case, all of the subjects noted that both boys and men are dark-haired, brown-eyed, and strong. They play baseball and take out the garbage. Doctors, truck drivers, and police officers are men. Fourth and eighth graders added that males urinate standing up, are active and athletic. Eighth graders added being decisive and competitive to the male traits.

These descriptions provide a feel for the data, and they clearly signal the tendencies to differentially assign activities, occupations, and physical characteristics to the two sexes before assigning personality attributes. We turn now to a statistical analysis of these trends. We performed two Guttman scalogram analyses (see Chapter 4 and Anderson, 1966) on the data. The first used strict criteria for "passing" each level, and the second used somewhat less stringent criteria.

For the first, we required the subjects to correctly attribute each of the items in the category to the normatively stereotypical sex to receive a passing score. Note that it was possible for them to attribute these traits to the other sex, too; our interest in this analysis centered on assigning the attributes according to societally gender-typed ways. Thus, to receive credit for a pass, a child had to assign all of the female-associated activities (sews, gets dressed up, cooks) to females (girls or women) and all of the male-associated activities (stands while urinating, plays baseball, takes out garbage) to males (boys or men). The same procedure was applied to occupations, physical characteristics, and to the personality traits. This procedure meant that a pass required the gender-typing of six items for the three classifications of activities, occupations, and physical attributes, and of 16 personality traits.

On the basis of our previous work and the research of others (particularly Wehren & De Lisi, 1983), we predicted that physical characteristics would be acquired the earliest. These characteristics contain many of the cues used by children to attribute gender. We expected activities and occupations to be acquired next. Children are likely to see the two sexes engaging in various activities, including those related to occupations, in their own lives, on television, and to hear about these activities as they listen to books. Personality traits should be recognized the most slowly, if at all. Such traits are not immediately obvious. They must be inferred from the behavior of others, at least at an early age. If Williams and his colleagues (e.g., Williams & Best, 1982) are right that gender concepts about males are acquired before those about females, then the instrumental traits should be accurately assigned to males before the expressive traits are accurately assigned to females. Accordingly, we predicted the following order: physical attributes, activities, occupations, instrumental personality traits, expressive personality traits.

The results of the application of the Guttman scalogram analysis are given in Table 7.2. As can be seen from the table, one type of violation appeared: Children occasionally missed credit for activities, although they received credit for the two surrounding categories, physical activities and occupations. The problem with activities was that some children had difficulty with the item about urinating while standing. Both of these kinds of violations decreased with the ages of the rater and of the stimulus person. In terms of the major predictions, occupations were credited almost as often as physical abilities and more often than activities. Hence, sex patterning of physical activities and of occupations seems to be added to gender concepts at a fairly early age. Finally, only a limited number of raters received credit

Table 7.2. Guttman Scalogram Analysis for Rating of Child and Adult Stimulus Persons by Preschoolers and by Fourth- and Eighth-Graders, Strict Criteria

		Dimensions				Stimulus Persons					
						Raters					
						Children			Adults		
Physical Attributes	Activities	Occupations	Instrumental Personality	Expressive Personality		Preschool	4	8	Preschool	4	8
Predicted											
−	−	−	−	−		18	16	9	15	11	3
+	−	−	−	−		26	3	3	27	1	2
+	+	−	−	−		...	...	...	...	...	...
+	+	+	−	−		21	47	60	30	54	60
+	+	+	+	−		...	...	...	...	...	...
+	+	+	+	+		...	6	8	...	9	15
Violations											
+	−	+	−	−		15	8	...	8	5	...

Note: Each column is based on 80 observations.

for the personality categories, and no rater received credit for gender typing instrumental traits before expressive ones. Personality characteristics seem to be differentially applied to the two sexes later and with less facility than the other categories. Overall, the coefficients of reproducibility were .97 for ratings of children and .98 for ratings of adults.

We repeated the analysis with less strict criteria for passing. In this case, we dropped the number required for passing from six to five for physical attributes, activities, and occupations and dropped the number required for passing the personality characteristics from eight to two. Relaxing the criteria meant that the raters would not be held responsible for the urinating question under activities. This activity is more private than the others and may not qualify for the assumption of the public nature of activities that prompted our original predictions. The only rationale for the marked reduction of the personality performance was to give us a better chance to probe the sequence of acquiring even a few personality differentiators.

Table 7.3 tells us that physical attributes, activities, and occupations are acquired early; personality attributes come later, and then in limited numbers. The coefficients of reproducibility were still high, .98 for ratings of both children and adults.

Overall, the results of the Guttman scalogram analyses argue that there is a sequence of gender-related attributions of the various categories. The more public, obvious characteristics seem to become part of gender concepts before more hidden, internal ones, such as personality characteristics. We found no evidence to indicate that instrumental attributes are acquired before expressive ones.

To summarize the nonforced-choice results, the traits assigned to the two sexes increase with the age of the subjects and with the age of the stimulus person. The older subjects attribute more traits to the stimulus persons than do the younger subjects, and the older stimulus persons (the adults) are assigned more traits than the younger stimulus persons (the children). Further, when the composite scores are examined, we found no evidence of gender stereotyping until the eighth grade. More detailed analyses of the individual items showed that personality traits are added to the gender concepts after physical traits, activities, and occupations, and that some of these traits showed gender stereotyping. In fact, only seven of the 16 personality traits showed gender stereotyping, despite the choice of these traits because they typically show differences with adults.

These results are consistent with our view that obvious, external characteristics (activities, occupations) should become part of a gender concept before less obvious ones (personality characteristics). They are inconsistent with the notion that attributes that do not require perceptual shifts (e.g., personality traits) will be learned before those that do (e.g., activities), as proposed by Gouze and Nadelman (1980) and Wehren and De Lisi (1983).

Table 7.3. Guttman Scalogram Analysis for Rating of Child and Adult Stimulus Persons by Preschoolers and by Fourth- and Eighth-Graders, Relaxed Criteria

	Dimensions					Stimulus Persons					
	Physical Attributes	Activities	Occupations	Instrumental Personality	Expressive Personality	Children			Adults		
						Raters					
						Preschool	4	8	Preschool	4	8
Predicted	–	–	–	–	–	14	8	3	7	4	...
	+	–	–	–	–	2	...	...	2	...	...
	+	+	–	–	–	2	...	...	1	...	...
	+	+	+	+	–	27	23	15	30	8	4
	+	+	+	+	–	2	3	1	1	5	2
	+	+	+	+	+	21	41	61	33	55	70
Violations	+	–	+	–	–	8	2	...	5	2	...
	+	+	+	–	+	4	3	...	1	6	4

Note: Each column is based on 80 observations.

Gender-typing and Gender-stereotyping:
Evidence from Forced-Choices

We turn next to the forced-choice procedure. Before examining the evidence of gender-typing and gender-stereotyping, we need to compare the non-forced- and forced-choice procedures, because the latter may overestimate differential attribution of the traits (gender stereotyping), and underestimate the extent to which the sexes share traits. Obviously, with the forced-choice procedure, each characteristic must be assigned to males or to females. The nonforced-choice procedure gives the subjects the options of assigning characteristics to one, both, or neither of the sexes. Although the mandated choice for each trait required by the forced procedure would almost certainly yield more attributions than the absence of such a mandate in the nonforced-choice technique, the difference would not necessarily be statistically significant. Moreover, any attributional differences between the two procedures might vary with the age of the stimulus persons and with the age and sex of the subjects.

To compare the attributions of the forced- and nonforced-choice procedures, we began with the subject's first attribution. This attribution represents her or his first choice. Then, in a separate analysis (which tests a "suppression effect" due to the initial choice) we looked at the second choices. To make this clearer, let's review the procedures. For the first set of questions, the forced choice procedure requires the subject to decide whether the story describes either most females or most males. Only one choice is allowed. Next, after what amounts to affirming one sex and rejecting the other, the subject was asked if the other sex could have the trait. Subjects in the nonforced-choice procedure had the options of saying that both, one, or neither sex could have the trait.

The forced-choice procedure does seem to overestimate initial attributions, as we had suspected. For each age group, the forced condition yielded reliably more attributions than the nonforced-choice condition, $F_{\text{Preschool}}$ (1, 232) = 809.92, $p < .001$; $F_{\text{4th grade}}$ (1, 232) = 890.78, $p < .001$; $F_{\text{8th grade}}$ (1, 232) = 954.55, $p < .001$. This pattern appeared for both ages and sexes of stimulus persons. Even so, when rating children, preschoolers did not systematically attribute the traits above a chance level (see the upper part of Figure 7.2).

The next question is whether the forced-choice procedure *underestimates* claims that both sexes may possess the characteristics. This set of analyses examined responses to the second queries, the entries in the lower part of Figure 7.2. This time we found below-chance assignments under the forced-choice procedure for the preschoolers and the fourth graders, but not for the eighth graders. Such below-chance responding is consistent with a suppression effect. Apparently, preschoolers and fourth graders find it difficult to change from their initial classification to another one, an effect observed

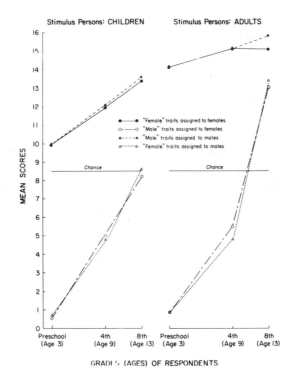

Figure 7.2   Mean gender-typing scores for four stimulus groups (girls, boys, women, men) by preschoolers, fourth- and eighth-graders, forced choice.

in other tasks with children (e.g., Cunningham & Odom, 1978; Medin, 1973; Smith, 1983), but the eighth graders are able to switch.

These analyses illustrate some different effects of the forced- and non-forced-choice procedures, but they do not tell us whether the two procedures yield different patterns of gender attributions. We already know the pattern for the nonforced-choice technique; now we examine it for the forced-choice procedure. As the right hand panel of Figure 7.2 indicates, the overall pattern for the forced-choice data was similar to that of the nonforced-choice data, except that the mean scores were higher for the former. The scores increased with the age of the respondent (from preschool to eighth grade), $F(1, 228) = 122.85$, $p < .001$, with the age of the stimulus person (from children to adults), $F(1, 228) = 562.93$, $p < .001$; but these increases were greater for preschoolers than for the eighth graders, yielding a significant interaction, $F(2, 228) = 25.81$, $p < .001$. Clearly, the forced-choice data suggested considerably more gender stereotyping than the nonforced-choice data. Perhaps the easiest and fastest way to grasp the differences in the results yielded by the two procedures is to compare Figures 7.1 and 7.2. They are like day and night. One striking difference is in the assignments of traits often associated with one or the other sex. With forced choice, these assignments were significantly below chance for the preschoolers and fourth graders and these assignments reached chance for the eighth graders. With unforced choice, these assignments were above chance for the fourth and eighth graders. In brief, the unforced choice seemed to permit the recognition that both sexes could have the same kinds of traits. But we still need information about the individual trait assignments under the forced choice regimen before drawing final conclusions.

To expand on this question, we scrutinized the responses to the individual traits. As with the nonforced-choice results, the personality traits became gender stereotypic at later ages than the other traits, and gender stereotyping increased with the ages of both the subjects and the stimulus persons. The forced-choice data differed from the nonforced-choice information in two ways: (a) the levels of attributions were higher and (b) gender stereotyping was reduced for the eighth graders compared to the fourth graders or the preschoolers. These comparisons support our contention that the forced-choice procedure may inflate estimates of gender stereotyping and they add the important qualifier that this inflation seems to have less effect with older subjects. The older, presumably more sophisticated subjects are more aware that both sexes could manifest various traits and are less likely to succumb to the "classification suppression effect" mentioned earlier.

Guttman scalogram analyses were applied to the forced-choice data. The conclusions were same as those from the nonforced-choice analyses.

Self Descriptions

With the self descriptions, children were asked to state whether or not each little story described the way they "really" were. Their answers gave us estimates of self concepts that could be compared with the concepts for others. In general, the children were accurate in describing their own physical characteristics, as Table 7.4 indicates. They knew what color hair they had, how long their hair was, and whether it was straight or curly. They knew what color eyes they had. Thus, these aspects, which we assume as part of their self schemata, were already well developed in the preschoolers.

Table 7.5 presents the percentages of respondents who claimed that they could engage in the activities and occupations and who said that they possessed various personality traits. These items were tallied as functions of their cultural stereotyping. Preschool girls were somewhat more likely than boys to claim stereotypic female occupations and activities, and the opposite effect appeared for boys, but these trends did not become statistically significant until the fourth grade. A similar pattern surfaced for some of the

Table 7.4.   Percentages of Children Accurately Describing Their Own Physical
Characteristics

	Preschool	4	8
		Grade of rater	
Hair length	99	100	100
Hair color	100	100	100
Hair style	99	100	100
Eye color	98	100	100

Table 7.5.   Percentages of Children Who Claimed That They Could Engage in
Various Activities and That They Possessed Various Personality Characteristics

	Grade and Sex of Rater					
	Preschool		4th		8th	
	F	M	F	M	F	M
Activities						
Female-associated	63	58	80	40	95	38
Male-associated	60	65	51	87	49	94
Occupations						
Female-associated	71	48	83	30	98	10
Male-associated	38	76	42	100	50	100
Personality traits						
Expressive	22	24	34	31	47	35
Instrumental	17	25	29	42	25	59

personality traits. Interestingly, self-endorsements of these traits were quite
low, reaching only 59% for boys proclaiming that they possessed male-associated traits. The counterpart figure for girls was 47%. Another interesting
trend was the tendency for more girls than boys to endorse personality traits
commonly associated with the other sex. In general, boys were more likely
to endorse being athletic and being active than the other instrumental traits.
Girls showed the same pattern, but to a lesser extent. With expressive traits,
however, girls were most likely to endorse being kind, warm, and considerate; boys preferred being understanding. These details, coupled with the
evidence of Table 7.5, inform us that both sexes of our respondents were
not only aware that both sexes could possess both expressive and instrumental traits; many of them also thought that they themselves represented
both types of attributes.

The principal differences between the self descriptions of personality
traits and those ascribed to others were that subjects of all ages claimed
fewer personality traits for themselves. These results suggest that personality
traits are not as prominent in self-concepts as in gender concepts for others.

Summing Up

How does all this information fit together? We have looked at different aspects of the data from different perspectives without collecting them into a unified whole. Now let us try to merge them, much as we might fit together the individual pieces of a large jigsaw puzzle. The most efficient first step toward this amalgamation is to list the major findings.

1. Physical traits, activities, and occupations are gender-typed at earlier ages than personality traits.
2. Adults are gender-typed more than children.
3. Adults are gender-stereotyped, whereas if children are gender-stereotyped, it is to a lesser extent. Under the nonforced-choice procedure, when subjects have an opportunity to attribute traits to one, both, or none of the sexes, children typically were not gender-stereotyped; under the forced-choice technique, children were more likely to be gender-stereotyped.
4. The tendencies to gender-type and to gender-stereotype increase with age.
5. Children's physical self-descriptions are accurate. Self descriptions of personality traits become increasingly stereotyped with age, but are not as stereotyped as attributions to adults.
6. Our respondents had delineated gender concepts about the characteristics typically attributed to both sexes in the culture. Concepts about males were acquired no earlier than concepts about females.

All of the above findings suggest that gender concepts change with age, not only in the kinds of traits or characteristics embodied in the concepts, but also with respect to the people to whom they are applied.

Let's assume, for the moment, that endorsement of the tested traits provides a window to the contents of gender concepts. If so, the stories from both the nonforced- and the forced-choice data have some similar themes.

The first common theme, that older children gender-type more than younger ones, suggests that traits are added to the gender concepts as the children age. Our data imply that traits or items are added to the concepts throughout the age range from three to 13, although we cannot estimate the rate of acquisition of the components.

The second theme, that more traits are assigned to adults than to children, implies that adults are perceived as more gender-typed than children are. This may be because adults, rather than children, tend to be used as the models for gender-defining behavior.

The third general result was that physical traits, occupations, and activities are gender-typed before personality traits. This is not surprising, for the physical differences between the sexes may be easier to perceive than the more elusive, less salient behavioral manifestations of personality traits. In addition, the imbalances of sexes in certain occupations are so extreme that this knowledge would be expected to enter gender concepts at an early age. Thus, even young children should observe that most truck drivers are men and most secretaries are women. These results appear to conflict with the nonsignificant differences for personality traits, physical appearance, and activities found by Wehren and De Lisi (1983), but they used a forced-choice procedure that may have reduced the sensitivity of their design.

The fourth theme is that the self concepts are not identical to concepts for others of the same sex or for concepts for others of the opposite sex. In general, our subjects accurately described their own physical characteristics, so the gender-typed hair and eye attributions did not reflect either a misunderstanding of these items or a lack of knowledge. The youngsters assumed that they could engage in various traditionally gender-typed activities and occupations, showing some tendency toward gender-stereotyping that did not become statistically significant until the fourth grade. The pattern for the personality traits was similar, except that markedly fewer personality traits showed gender differences, even at the eighth grade. Taken together, these results suggest that the self-concept does not contain as pronouncedly gender-stereotyped information as the other, the cultural gender concepts. We were not prepared for this finding, because previous studies in our laboratory and the work of Spence, Helmreich, and Stapp (1975) suggested that self concepts would show greater *diversity* than cultural gender concepts, even for the same gender. This work was conducted with college students, however, leading us to suspect additional changes in the self schema from the eighth grade to adulthood.

Overall, the results produce a picture of an increasingly finely tuned process of concept generation, a process that fashions gradually accruing, culturally-reflective gender concepts. The data lead us toward the conclusion that gender concepts begin as constellations of attributes associated with adults. Initially, these constellations are fragmentary and not necessarily accurate. In time, more attributes are added, and the constellations become increasingly similar to culturally held beliefs about the two sexes (which does not guarantee accuracy, of course). Extrapolations to children also are developmentally delayed.

Although the two techniques produced the common themes just discussed, they yielded some differences, as well. One marked difference was that responding was lower under the nonforced-choice regimen than under the forced-choice one. A second difference was that more gender-typing appeared with the nonforced-choice procedure than with the forced-choice one, but the converse held for gender-stereotyping.

The lower responding under nonforced- and under forced-choice conditions suggested that the subjects sometimes thought that neither sex had the characteristic. The nonforced-choice procedure gave them the opportunity to indicate this belief, whereas the forced-choice procedure did not.

The differences in gender-typing and gender-stereotyping expressed through the two procedures were pronounced. The nonforced-choice data suggested that the fourth and eighth graders thought that both sexes could have most of the tested traits. Preschoolers assigned these traits to both sexes at a chance level. The forced-choice data indicated that both pre-schoolers and fourth graders assigned female-related traits to females and male-related traits to males, whereas the eighth graders were more likely to indicate that both sexes could have both female- and male-related character-istics. Lohaus and Trautner (in press) found similar results.

Before we probe the meaning of these results still further, it is reasonable to inquire more about the two testing procedures themselves. We used the nonforced procedure to give the subjects more latitude to indicate that one, both, or neither of the sexes could have the traits. The forced-choice task requires that children select one and only one sex for each trait, thereby assuring a high level of responding. Is the result an overestimation of gen-der-consistent attributions and an underestimation of gender-inconsistent attributions? Such an underestimation could be produced by difficulty chil-dren have in changing from one classification to another, (e.g., Medin, 1973; Smith, 1983). The data of Figure 7.2 are consistent with this interpre-tation. But it is also possible that the two techniques really test different questions. The nonforced-choice procedure may test the child's own beliefs about gender roles, whereas the forced-choice approach tests the child's knowledge of cultural mores. Thus, the child may know about the cultural expectations for the two sexes and be able to respond accordingly in the forced-choice format, but this knowledge does not necessarily indicate en-dorsement of these expectations. This interpretation seems unlikely because the two-step format clearly distinguished between one person and most people of a particular sex, and this was true for both procedures. Moreover, the children's spontaneous comments following both of the procedures in-dicated that they were telling us about cultural gender roles.

There is one additional methodological question to consider: the yea-saying bias. Although this tendency might have been present, the discerning responses in the nonforced condition discount this argument. The nonforced condition required the children to decide whether a woman (man, girl, boy) would or would not participate in the activity, thereby providing more lati-tude than the forced-choice condition. The greater sensitivity of the non-forced condition is reflected in the more discriminating results.

One other reason the forced-choice technique might have produced un-duly strong evidence of gender-typing is that youngsters frequently refuse to shift from one categorization scheme to another (e.g., Cunningham & Odom, 1978; Medin, 1973; Smith, 1983). This explanation predicts that subjects in the forced-choice situation would deny that the other sex could exhibit the behavior once they had assigned the behavior to a particular sex. This prediction was supported for young subjects (preschool and fourth grade) but not for the older ones (eighth grade). Thus, the explanation for why earlier investigations found strong evidence of gender stereotyping among young children seems to be that the use of a simple forced-choice technique dissuaded the young subjects from stating that the other sex also could enter into the activity.

The tendency of the forced-choice technique to produce strong evidence of gender typing may well explain why Williams et al. (1975) found more pronounced gender-typing than we did. They relied exclusively on a forced-choice procedure. Another methodological difference was that their adjectives, drawn from a modified adjective check list, differed from ours. To test the adjective-difference possibility, we compared the results for four adjectives used in both sets of experiments (emotional, gentle, independent, and self-confident). Our results for these adjectives mirrored theirs. It seems unlikely, therefore, that the differences in the results can be attributed solely to the use of different trait-adjectives. More likely, in our opinion, is the explanation that their scores were inflated by reliance in the forced-choice technique.

Reliable evidence that gender-stereotyping increases with age is consistent with most models of gender development (e.g., Kohlberg, 1966; Martin & Halverson, 1981; Mischel, 1970). Our results further imply that even fourth-grade children believe that most people, regardless of gender, have both expressive and instrumental traits, a sophistication that is not emphasized by the extant models of gender-role development.

The results have practical significance as well as theoretical importance. If youngsters generally assume that adults of both sexes can engage in the tested behaviors, then a task for society may be to continue to support these beliefs and attributions rather than to encourage children to dichotomize their conceptions of "appropriate" gender-role behavior. As Ashmore and Del Boca (1979) contend, gender stereotypes may be viewed as sets of inferential relations that link attributes with the social categories of female and male. These linkages constrain both perceivers and the perceived, since most members of a culture are likely to share similar gender stereotypes. Such constraints on the interactions of individuals may function as self-fulfilling prophecies that curtail both personal and interpersonal development.

CHAPTER 8

Gender-Role Identity and Adjustment

We shift now from explorations of the contents of gender concepts to potential applications of them. As argued in Chapter 1, one reason to be interested in gender concepts is because these concepts may guide our behavior. Included in the attitudes and beliefs encoded into gender concepts may be the notion that it is more appropriate, in some sense, or more adaptive to behave in ways that accord with societally defined gender roles. Is this true? What is the relation between gender roles and social effectiveness? In this chapter, we consider one kind of social effectiveness, adjustment. Adjustment is usually related to mental health, an area that has become a favorite of some students of gender roles.

The last decade has seen a major change in the psychological concepts of gender-role identity and their relation to mental health. Traditionally, masculinity and femininity were considered to be opposite ends of a single continuum with the consequent assumption that a trade-off existed between femininity and masculinity. To the extent that one became more feminine, one necessarily and compensatorily became less masculine, and vice versa. Included in these conceptions of masculinity and femininity was the idea that traditional sex-typing, masculinity in the male and femininity in the female, contributed to mental health, whereas cross-gender typing was maladaptive (see discussions in Baumrind, 1982; Bem, 1975; Kaplan, 1979; Spence, Helmreich, & Stapp, 1975; Taylor & Hall, 1982). The ideal toward which one should strive was to be a feminine woman or a masculine man, and parents were routinely warned that children who failed to acquire these concepts would suffer from inadequacies, inabilities to adjust, and other dread disabilities. These prescriptions were consistent with Freud's view, of course, for he, like most of his followers, believed that a key to adjustment was the acquisition of a gender role typically associated with one's sex.

137

More recently, investigators, disappointed by measures of masculinity and femininity and skeptical of theories that minimized the vast overlap of abilities and traits in the two sexes, began to challenge the psychoanalytic dictum. They have proposed that masculinity and femininity represent independent dimensions (Bem, 1974; Constantinople, 1973; Spence & Helmreich, 1978; Spence et al., 1975). Thus, a person could possess both feminine and masculine personality traits. The term psychological androgyny has been used to describe persons who manifest high levels of both masculine (instrumental) and feminine (expressive) traits. I will use the term androgyny in most of this chapter to maintain comparability with the literature. It is important to note, however, that this term is undesirable from a number of perspectives. Androgyny is not always related to behavior it should predict (Taylor & Hall, 1982). Androgyny is currently estimated from tests that contain (a) instrumental (masculine) items which primarily assess achievements and accomplishments and (b) expressive (feminine) items which primarily concern feelings. The areas hardly seem broad enough to encompass gender-associated attributes. This problem is directly related to another: the notion that the concept of androgyny necessarily assumes that the scales from which it is derived are real, reliable, and valid (Bem, 1981). These assumptions have little empirical support. Moreover, androgyny proscribes additional behavior demands on both sexes. It posits that we need to develop both expressive and instrumental traits. Finally, and most troublesome in my opinion, is that additional emphasis conferred on the views that some traits are most often associated with one sex than the other, despite contradictory evidence. As I will argue in the discussion, my own view is that it makes more sense—and is more consistent with the literature—to postulate that there are a wide variety of traits that may be useful under certain situations. Most people presumably possess these characteristics to a greater or lesser degree. It then follows that a model of flexibility would have the most promise for mental health.

Along with the model of androgyny came a new model of mental health. This model held that traditional gender roles may be maladaptive, limiting the behavior and growth of the individual. Androgynous roles presumably offer the flexibility of a more diverse response repertoire and may, if the behaviors were selected appropriately, be more adaptive. As part of an effort to resolve these issues, scales such as the Bem Sex Role Inventory (BSRI; Bem, 1974) and the Personal Attributes Questionnaire (PAQ; Spence, et al., 1975) were developed. The scales have been used to identify the extent to which individuals are masculine-typed (high degree of masculine traits, low degree of feminine traits) or feminine-typed (high degree of feminine traits, low degree of masculine traits). They also have been used to identify two other groups: the androgynous (high degree of both masculine and feminine traits) and the undifferentiated (low degree of both masculine and feminine traits).

An androgyny model predicts better psychological adjustment among androgynous women and men than among traditionally sex-typed people for, as Silvern and Ryan (1979, p. 740) state, "Androgynous persons should be maximally flexible, free to respond appropriately to situations regardless of whether they call for traditionally masculine or feminine traits or behaviors." The traditionally sex-typed individual is not as adept in situations calling for cross-gender behaviors.

Studies have demonstrated that, in at least some situations, androgynous individuals show more behavioral flexibility than traditionally sex-typed individuals (Bem, 1975; Bem & Lenney, 1976; Major, Carnevale, & Deaux, 1981; Orlofsky & Windle, 1978). Androgynous persons were more adaptable in cross-gender situations than traditionally sex-typed persons. Thus, the androgyny model has some support in terms of behavioral flexibility. In all these studies, androgyny has been defined by high endorsement of both female-related (expressive) and male-related (instrumental) traits. These results seem eminently reasonable and must be true in the extreme. Consider, for example, the situation in which one has a flat tire on a deserted stretch of an interstate highway. An adaptive response is to change the tire. Presumably changing the tire requires competence and independence, and this is true regardless of one's sex. Similarly, to be successful in a position that involves extensive contact with the public, it is helpful to be pleasant, kind, responsive—all attributes that are stereotypically associated with women. Nonetheless, all of the attributes should also benefit men in such situations.

Despite the reasonableness of the model of flexible responding, concordant results are not always found, however, as Taylor and Hall (1982) note in a review of relevant literature. For example, when self-report or self-esteem was used as a measure of mental health, Deutsch and Gilbert (1976) found that androgynous women described themselves as better adjusted than did traditionally sex-typed women, but traditionally sex-typed men described themselves as better adjusted than androgynous men. They concluded that masculinity predicted adjustment, not androgyny. Additionally, Silvern and Ryan (1979) found superior adjustment among androgynous women, but not among androgynous men. Other research using the BSRI has yielded no significant differences in the self-esteem of androgynous and masculine college students (Flaherty & Dusek, 1980; Kelly & Worell, 1977). In contrast, Spence, Helmreich and Stapp (1975), using their Personal Attributes Questionnaire (PAQ, Spence, et al., 1975), found that among college students, masculine-typed and feminine-typed persons had a less positive self-concept than androgynous persons. Spence et al. (1975) also noted that the traits previously labeled as masculine are more accurately called instrumental or agentic and the traits previously called feminine should be called expressive or communal. Taylor and Hall (1982) provide an excellent review of the literature.

Thus, a controversy exists in the literature on adult androgyny: Are high levels of self esteem and adjustment related to instrumentality (masculinity) or to the integration of both instrumental (masculine) and expressive (feminine) characteristics? Support for androgyny as a model of good adult mental health is mixed; the importance of high instrumentality seems clear, but the importance of high expressiveness is less clear.

Research on children and adolescents, although scarce, yields similar findings. Hall and Halberstadt (1980) found that a high level of instrumentality was associated with a positive self-concept among elementary age children. In adolescents, Spence and Helmreich (1978) found that both instrumentality and expressiveness showed a strong positive relationship with self-esteem for both males and females. Massad (1981) found that in the adolescent, androgyny was associated with better adjustment than traditional sex-typing among females, but not among males.

Note that the foregoing research emphasized correlations between individuals' own scores on gender-typed trait scales and ratings of their adjustment. Perceptions of peers have not been examined, despite their potential impact on mental health. For example, peers may reject or accept an individual as adjusted or competent because of their perceptions of the individual's gender-related traits. An androgyny model of mental health predicts that peers should perceive well adjusted peers as combining high levels of both instrumental and expressive traits within their personalities. Poorly adjusted peers should be perceived as gender-typed or undifferentiated. A traditional model predicts that peers should perceive well adjusted peers as gender-typed and perceive poorly adjusted peers as possessing cross-gender traits. These predictions motivated Mariam Zaknoen (1983) to conduct the described research as her honors project at Indiana University.

Her primary purpose was to examine perceptions of the traits assigned to other people who are considered adjusted or maladjusted. She asked, "Are individuals who are considered well-adjusted also perceived to have high levels of instrumental traits, expressive traits, or both? And are poorly adjusted peers perceived as having the opposite configuration of traits?" An androgyny model implies that high levels of both instrumentality and expressiveness would be associated with better adjustment, whereas traditional gender-typing models of psychological adjustment predict that well-adjusted females would have a high level of expressiveness but not instrumentality and well-adjusted males would have the opposite configuration. A flexibility model makes the same predictions as the androgyny model, in that individuals with many skills (traits) are more likely to adjust successfully to different situations than those with fewer skills (traits) but these traits are not necessarily tied to instrumentality and expressiveness.

A secondary purpose was to investigate perceptions of the relation between gender-role identity and adjustment in three age groups: childhood, early adolescence, and early adulthood. These perceptions presumably affect the generation of gender concepts. If the individual's cultural concept for her or his own sex includes specific adjustment-related traits, these traits also may be incorporated into the personal schema and used to channel experiences. For example, the girl who thinks that most well-adjusted females are both warm and independent may include these traits in her self-concept. If so, her self-concept will sensitize her to situations calling for warmth and independence.

Perceptions of the relation between certain traits and adjustments found in cultural gender concepts function as a kind of social stereotype. These stereotypes constitute social demands that presumably operate in children and adults. Thus, children as well as adults are pressured by peers and the media to conform to social stereotypes. Costanzo (1970) found that pressure to conform to social stereotypes seems to be greatest in childhood and early adolescence. It decreases in late adolesence and early adulthood. Failure to conform to social stereotypes in childhood and early adolescence may affect psychological and social adjustment. While the androgynous person may be seen as deviating from traditional gender roles, the acquisition of a second set of valuable traits could be beneficial and may outweigh any negative consequences of deviating from social stereotypes (Massad, 1981). If an androgyny model of mental health is supported, androgyny will be related to adjustment in all age groups with the strongest relationship in early adulthood when the pressures to conform are not as strong. If a traditional model is supported traditional gender-typing should be associated with better adjustment in all age groups.

Specifically, Zaknoen (1983) asked subjects to describe well adjusted and poorly adjusted peers in terms of instrumental and expressive personality characteristics, as measured by the PAQ.

Two hundred and eighteen students (113 females and 105 males) participated in the study. The sample consisted of 60 (30 female and 30 male) fourth-grade students, 73 (43 female and 30 male) ninth-grade students, and 85 (40 female and 45 male) college students. The fourth graders were from two elementary schools in a midwestern city. Incomes at these schools were low-average to average. The ninth graders were from the two high schools in the same city. College students were undergraduates at Indiana University who participated for credit in a course requirement.

Spence and Helmreich's Personal Attributes Questionnaire and the Children's Personal Attributes Questionnaire (CPAQ; Hall & Halberstadt, 1980) were used. The CPAQ was developed from the PAQ and corresponds item-by-item to the PAQ, except that the PAQ is scored on a 5-point scale from 0-4 and CPAQ usually is scored on a 4-point scale from 1-4. We equated the two for experimental comparisons. In each case, the items are presented as bipolar adjectives such as "Not at all aggressive... Very aggressive." The anchoring adjectives are numbered 0 and 4. The subject selects the number that best represents how descriptive the trait is of the group being rated.

The short versions of the PAQ and the CPAQ were used, each containing 24 personality characteristics or attributes. The questionnaires contain three scales: a masculine scale (M^+), a feminine scale (F^+), and a masculinity-femininity (M-F) scale. The M^+ and F^+ scales contain attributes that are socially desirable for both sexes, but are associated more with one sex (i.e., attributes on the M^+ scale are associated more with males and attributes on the F^+ scale are associated more with females). The items on the M^+ scale constitute instrumental traits, the items on the F^+ scale constitute expressive traits. The attributes on the M-F scale were judged to be differentially socially desirable for the two sexes (e.g., aggressiveness is desirable in males, whereas nonaggressiveness is desirable in females).

Children used the CPAQ and college students, the PAQ, to describe a well-adjusted male and female or a poorly-adjusted male and female from their peer group. Half of the males and half of the females described both a well-adjusted male and a well-adjusted female. The rest described both a poorly-adjusted male and a poorly-adjusted female. Each subject thus completed the PAQ or CPAQ twice, once for a female and once for a male. Subjects were asked to think of only one female peer and one male peer and answer all questions describing these peers. One half of the subjects described a female first and then a male, the other half described a male first and then a female. Classes were randomly assigned to either the well-adjusted or the poorly-adjusted condition. Differences between classes in each condition were minimal. Instructions were on the first page of each test and were read aloud by the experimenter. A summary of the instructions for each condition is as follows: Well-adjusted condition—"Think about one of your classmates who can be described in this way. Someone who can handle changes and problems that come up in life, who gets along with others and who is happy with and likes himself or herself. Think about a classmate who is like this and answer the questions describing this person." Poorly-adjusted condition—"Think about one of your classmates who can be described in this way. Someone who has trouble handling changes and problems that come up in life, who has trouble getting along with others and does not like himself or herself. Think about a classmate who is like this and answer the questions describing this person."

The sex of the respondent did not affect any comparisons, indicating that both sexes agreed on most of the ratings assigned the well- and poorly-adjusted stimulus persons. This result documents the consistency with which we learn and internalize socially stereotypic views. Because the sex of the respondent did not differentially affect the data, this variable will not be discussed further.

The results will be considered in terms of the descriptions of the female stimulus persons and of the male stimulus persons. We then move to the levels of instrumental and expressive scores assigned to the stimulus persons.

Descriptions of Female Stimulus Persons

Across all grades the well-adjusted female was attributed significantly more expressive (F$^+$) traits, $F(1, 202) = 30.80$, $p < .01$, and more instrumental (M$^+$) traits, $F(1, 203) = 28.21$, $p < .01$, than the poorly-adjusted female, as shown in Figures 8.1 and 8.2. These results support the androgyny model of adjustment.

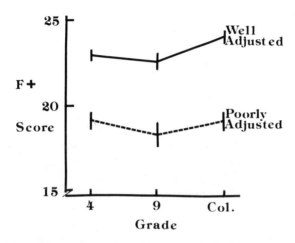

Figure 8.1 Mean F$^+$ scores attributed to well adjusted and to poorly adjusted female peers.

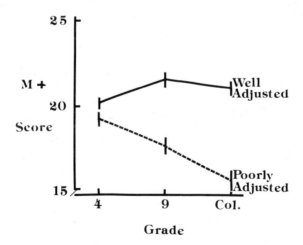

Figure 8.2 Mean M$^+$ scores attributed to well adjusted and poorly adjusted female peers.

In addition, adjustment interacted with grades, $F(2, 203) = 92.60, p < .05$, for the instrumental (M$^+$) traits. This interaction occurred because the M$^+$ score increased with age for the well-adjusted females but decreased with age for the poorly-adjusted females (see Figure 8.1). The well-adjusted and poorly-adjusted females were not described significantly differently on the M-F$^+$ scale, nor did these scores change with age.

In effect, the participants were telling us that the female peers whom they thought were well adjusted combined such traits as being warm, gentle, aware of the feelings of others, with those of being competent, active, and similar attributes. Moreover, the peers perceived to be well adjusted were assigned more of these characteristics than those female peers who were seen as poorly adjusted.

Descriptions of Male Stimulus Persons

For all three grades, in comparison to poorly-adjusted males, the well-adjusted males were attributed significantly more expressive (F$^+$) traits, $F(1, 202) = 69.78$, $p < .01$, and more instrumental (M$^+$) traits, $F(1,202) = 47.91$, $p < .01$ (Figure 8.4), corroborating the adjustment model.

Adjustment and grade again interacted, $F(2, 203) = 4.64$, $p < .01$. The expressive scores increased with age for the well-adjusted males and decreased with age for the poorly-adjusted males, as shown in Figure 8.3. The well-adjusted male was attributed significantly more instrumental (M$^+$) traits

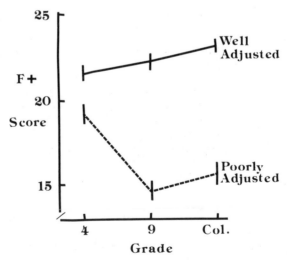

Figure 8.3   Mean F$^+$ scores attributed to well adjusted and to poorly adjusted male peers.

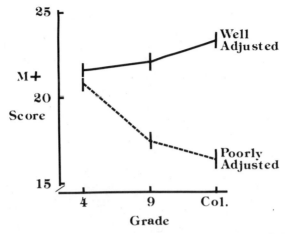

Figure 8.4   Mean M$^+$ scores attributed to well adjusted and poorly adjusted male peers.

as age increased and the poorly-adjusted male was assigned fewer instrumental (M$^+$) traits with age (Figure 8.4). The well-adjusted males also received higher M-F scores than the poorly-adjusted males, $F(1,203) = 15.21, p < .01$.

According to the results about male peers, it was almost as though the peers seen as well adjusted were assigned increasing abilities to be warm, sensitive to others, whereas the peers considered to be poorly adjusted were attributed decreasing awareness of and sensitivity toward others. A similar pattern emerged with the more instrumental traits, suggesting that peers seen as well adjusted were simply granted more distinctive, positive traits of all kinds. The converse held for the peers seen as poorly adjusted, almost as if they were becoming less colorful or distinctive.

Levels of Instrumental and Expressive Scores Assigned to Females and Males

The preceding results are consistent with the androgyny model of adjustment, but they don't compare the attributions to male and female stimulus persons who were considered well- or poorly-adjusted. Accordingly, we examined the differences in the levels of instrumental and expressive traits given each gender at each grade. Across all grades the well-adjusted males received similarly high levels of both instrumental and expressive traits. For the poorly-adjusted males, no significant differences were found in the levels of instrumental and expressive traits for the fourth grade and college, but ninth graders assigned significantly fewer expressive traits than instrumental traits, $t(36) = 2.8, p < .01$.

Thus, well-adjusted males were considered both expressive and instrumental, whereas poorly-adjusted males had lower levels, and their expressiveness, in particular was seen as considerably lower by the ninth graders. For the well-adjusted female, significantly more expressive than instrumental traits were assigned by both the fourth graders, t (22) = 2.18, $p < .05$, and the college students, t (40) = 3.0, $p < .01$. The well-adjusted ninth graders were attributed equal levels of instrumental and expressive traits. In the poorly-adjusted condition, college females were attributed significantly fewer instrumental traits than expressive traits, t (41) = 2.51, $p < .05$. No significant differences were found for the fourth and ninth grade poorly adjusted females. Well-adjusted females were seen as having high levels of expressive and instrumental traits. Poorly-adjusted females received lower levels of these traits, particularly instrumental ones (at the adult level).

Summing Up

The present study contrasted a traditional model of gender-role identity and adjustment with an androgyny model. A traditional model predicts that well-adjusted individuals will possess characteristics typically associated with their gender, whereas poorly-adjusted persons possess cross-gender traits. An androgyny model predicts that well-adjusted males and females possess both instrumental and expressive traits.

In all grades well-adjusted females were described as possessing instrumental traits to a greater degree than poorly-adjusted females, a result that supports an androgyny model. These differences also increased with age. As age of the subjects increased more instrumental traits were assigned to the well-adjusted female, and the importance of instrumental traits for good adjustment became stronger. As age of the subjects increased, fewer instrumental traits were assigned to the poorly-adjusted females. Moreover, well-adjusted females were described as possessing expressive traits to a greater degree than poorly-adjusted females. Well-adjusted females were thus described by their peers as having higher levels of both instrumental and expressive traits than the poorly-adjusted females. This balance was the strongest in the ninth grade, where there were no significant differences in levels of instrumental and expressive traits assigned to peers perceived as well-adjusted.

Similarly, in all grades well-adjusted males were described as possessing expressive traits to a greater degree than poorly-adjusted males, a result that supports an androgyny model. These differences also increased with age. Older age groups of subjects assigned more expressive traits to the well-adjusted males, suggesting that the importance of expressive traits for good adjustment became stronger. The poorly adjusted males were attributed fewer expressive traits as age increased. Well-adjusted males also received more instrumental traits than poorly-adjusted males. For all grades the levels of instrumental and expressive traits given to the well-adjusted males did not differ significantly. Peers perceived well-adjusted males as possessing both instrumental and expressive traits. Better adjustment in males was not related to high instrumentality only, as a traditional model would predict, but was related to high expressiveness in addition to high instrumentality.

What do these results portend for various models of gender roles? Before attempting to answer this question, I must enter an essential caveat. The current research considered *perceptions* of well-adjusted and poorly-adjusted people; it did not study the traits actually possessed by such people. It would be instructive to bring together these two lines of research, since perceptions of the well-adjusted and of the poorly-adjusted are likely to guide behavior toward them; behavior which, in turn, may influence the actions of the targeted individuals.

The present findings support what has been called "androgyny" as a model of good mental health. Persons who have the capabilities of using both instrumental and expressive traits, when situationally appropriate, regardless of gender, should have the potential to adjust more readily to the many diverse situations encountered in daily life. As individuals get older the benefits of androgny seem to become more apparent. With traditional gender-roles changing, gender-typed individuals may find it difficult to adjust to current situations that require competence in a mixture of attributes stereotypically divided between the sexes.

This view of the relation between gender-roles and mental health differs markedly from the traditional model espoused by Freud, many of his followers, and even by some proponents of social learning and cognitive-developmental theories. Associating gender-stereotypic attitudes with good adjustment, the traditional view also has been promulgated by many therapists. While our research and that of others does not deny the value of developing gender concepts with traditional cultural components and of incorporating at least some of the components from the like-sex concept into the self-concept, they strongly argue that children perceive and appreciate the utility of being able to use situationally-appropriate expressive *and* instrumental behaviors.

Is there an alternative to androgyny theory? I think so. The essence of androgyny theory, which I suspect accounts for its successes, as well as the findings that "masculinity" predicts adjustment either as effectively or more effectively than androgyny, is that the possession of diverse attributes contributes to mental health, just as certain attributes contribute to success (or failure) in any human endeavor. Some ingredients for mental health in a complex culture such as ours are not difficult to identify. These components of self-esteem, self-respect, and the feeling of being in control, of being important to others, of being needed are all significant. What attributes are likely to contribute to these components of mental health? The abilities to be independent, warm, competent, sensitive, decisive... These are not traits that are the province of one sex and not the other. These are traits of the human condition, traits that serve well in many circumstances, regardless of sex. When individuals, be they male or female, have difficulty manifesting these traits in situations which summon them, these inabilities would be expected to threaten their perceptions of themselves as being independent, warm, competent, and so on, and their mental health may be made vulnerable, as a consequence.

Let us consider an illustration. Mary has just moved into a new neighborhood, and she wants to be a part of a group of children who play field hockey. They ignore her, because she knows nothing about the game. What should she do? There are various possibilities, including looking for other friends, but she really wants to play with the field hockey players. She decides to learn to play. This takes time, the determination to practice, the possible postponement of other things she would like to do, but in the end, she knows that she did what she set out to do, to learn to play field hockey. Chances are that she will be accepted. Even if she isn't, her efforts are likely to enhance self-esteem and self-respect. If she had chosen another route, that of feeling sorry for herself and becoming a recluse, it is less clear that her behavior would have had the same salutary effects on her mental health.

As Mary moved toward her goal of becoming a field hockey player, she was manifesting courage, independence, competence, the ability to make up her mind, perseveration, and so forth—all abilities that may be possessed by both males and females. Neither sex has a stronger claim on these abilities than the other one.

What I am arguing, as a resolution to the apparent discrepancies in the literature between the forces heralding androgyny as the new mental health panacea and those proclaiming masculinity, is that both are wrong in their underlying assumptions about the ascriptions of traits to one sex more than to the other. All that is needed as a corrective is to shift the emphasis from a gender-based to an individual-based ascription of attributes. Such an approach would resolve the androgyny-masculinity difference about mental health by assuming that individuals who are able to employ relevant abilities as appropriate to the situation are more likely to be adaptable and to function in a mentally healthy way than individuals who are less able to summon these abilities. The task is then to identify the abilities, which, as I implied above, include independence, warmth, competence, sensitivity, and so forth. This approach, which I will call a model of flexibility, has the added advantage of not perpetuating suspect, demonstrably inaccurate, and potentially damaging beliefs that the two sexes differ substantially in personality characteristics.

from *I'm Not for Women's Lib . . . But*, copyright bülbül 1976, Arachne
Publishing, Mountain View, CA. 94040

CHAPTER 9

Gender Concepts: Retrospect and Prospect

A friend of mine took her 3-year-old daughter to the local shopping mall to buy some presents. Spying a heavily bearded man with long, flowing locks, she asked loudly, in a puzzled voice, "Mommy, why does that lady have a beard?"

This tale from the "real world" spendidly corroborates our research in the laboratory. In this chapter, we plan to integrate our findings with speculations about their implications. First, however, we will examine the structure of gender concepts identified by the research. This aim is most easily satisfied by relating various themes of the book to relevant predictions from the theories. Another aim is to develop the cognitive gender model, and to discuss some of its implications. We begin with some of the central themes, the questions raised by theories of gender development.

Are Gender Concepts Genital Concepts?

Psychoanalytic theory revolves around the penis and its psychological meaning to the individual. Those with penises (males) fear its loss (castration) by their fathers, who are seen as rivals for the love of their mothers. Males supposedly renounce their affiliation with their mothers, turning instead to an identification with their fathers. Those without penises (females), already "castrated," seek penises through an identification with their fathers. This forbidden activity must be replaced by an association with their mothers. Women do not seek to have their own penis—rather they seek its substitute in the form of pregnancy. Thus, the presence or absence of the penis is an essential element in psychoanalytic theory and should, therefore, be prominent in gender concepts.

The presence of a penis also may have a pronounced social significance, since social and cultural power typically resides with males. Males may be envied, imitated, venerated, because they possess this inferred badge of superiority. This view led Kessler and McKenna (1978) to postulate the existence of a "cultural penis," one that is assumed to exist for persons considered male. A cultural penis may be inferred even when a person is clothed or when the actual genitals differ from the deduced ones (as may occur with transsexuals). This cultural penis model predicts that the correlates of a cultural penis, male-related characteristics, should be preeminent. These characteristics are the standard against which individuals judge the gender of others. If male-related characteristics are present, the person is a male. If the characteristics are absent, the person is a female. Although these models do not deny the possibility of forming concepts about female-related characteristics, the availability of these concepts is not necessary for the operation of the processes hypothesized by the models. The only set of concepts that is required is the male-related one.

Both the psychoanalytic and the cultural penis models predict that the penis and male-related cues will be particularly important in gender attribution. As we noted repeatedly in discussing our experimental results, we found no evidence that children use genitals or even overall body contours as gender markers. These cues may aid adults, but they do not appear to influence the ability of children to identify gender. This result occurred throughout our testing with children's own drawings, pictures, and videotapes of children and adults. Thus, the psychoanalytic insistence on the importance of the penis to the development of gender schemata received no verification from our data. Further, our respondents had concepts about female-related characteristics that were as well developed as those for male-related ones.

Adults add a genital component to their gender-concepts, but their gender concepts also contain far more than the notion of a societally-venerated, societally-valued penis for males and the absence of this object for females. Presumably, these concepts developed from those they acquired as children, when their concepts were not genital concepts.

Are Gender Concepts Male Concepts?

The prediction that male-related cues would be particularly important stems from some linguistic considerations, in addition to the theoretical predictions just described. It appears that the pronoun "he" may be acquired somewhat earlier than the pronoun "she." Using an experimental technique that required both comprehension and production, Webster and Ingram (1972) found that the pronoun "he" was used correctly by most children aged three to three and one-half years, whereas the pronoun "she" was not used correctly by most children until they were four years or over. These estimates were taken from fairly small samples of 10 children in each age bracket, so we consider them to be tentative. According to Wells's (1985) naturalistic production data, "he" was used by at least 75% of 40-month-old children but the use of "she" was slower, not being used by 75% of the children until they were 55 months.

The prediction that male-associated cues would carry greater weight than female-associated cues received some limited, indirect support from our research. When head and clothing cues were obscured by paper bag hoods and capes in the first videotape experiment the subjects could not accurately identify gender. Under these conditions, they were more likely to guess "boy" than "girl," suggesting a male bias that could reflect a social importance and ascendancy assigned to males in our society. Further, the picture experiment data indicated that male-related cues were more limited and more rigidly defined than female-related cues. That is, when making gender attributions, the children said, "Boy," if the figure had short hair *and* had at least one other male-related characteristic (dark color or straight style). No single attribute was sufficient. Figures who deviated from this protocol were labeled as girls. On one interpretation, these results imply that the subjects used a tightly restricted protocol for maleness, perhaps because of the hypothetical cultural preeminence of this designation. This interpretation would be consistent with the psychoanalytic and cultural penis views.

But an alternative interpretation exists. The reader will recall that in the picture experiment the children said, "Girl" when any *one* of three hair cues (longer-than-chin length hair, curly hair, blonde hair) appeared. Thus, it could be argued that femaleness could be predicted from single cues, where maleness required at least two. If so, does this make femaleness the more important criterion? Which interpretation is correct? Is maleness such an important designation that it requires a number of verifying cues or is femaleness so easy to identify that single cues are sufficient? Although the two theoretical views appear to favor the former, a third interpretation reconciles the two in a way that accommodates both views and the experimental data, as well.

This third interpretation does not deny the importance of maleness, but proposes that maleness is defined as the absence of femaleness. This perspective, advanced by a number of researchers (David & Brannon, 1976; Farrell, 1974; Hartley, 1959; Pleck, 1981), claims that male roles are defined in opposition to female roles. In terms of psychoanalytic theory the use of female cues as a reference is reasonable, for males must learn to dissociate themselves from the identifications with their mothers, and females must ally themselves with their mothers. Both processes require knowledge of female-related characteristics. This third interpretation is consistent with some aspects of the cultural penis model, as well. Kessler and McKenna's (1978) model is based, in large measure, on the results of their experiment with adding parts of figures. When a penis was present, the figure usually was called a male even if other female characteristics appeared, and, when asked what could be done to make the figure the other sex, adding or deleting a penis was the common response. These results suggested that the penis or its conceptual equivalent was the *sine qua non* for maleness. Their subjects were adults. It seems plausible to assume that this equivalence of a cultural penis with maleness emerges as the gender concept develops. On this view, male-related cues first acquire their definition through contrasts with female-related cues.

Clearly, neither physical nor cultural penises appeared to be major cues to gender attribution in our experiments, thereby partially rebutting the psychoanalytic and cultural penis models. Through the addition of some assumptions, aspects of the models and the data can be reconciled. The central assumption that must be made is that female-related cues are equally or more important than male-related cues to gender attribution. This assumption is interesting, because it relates to other models, including the versions of psychoanalytic theory that stress the role of female caretakers in the child's early development (e.g., Horney, 1926; Chodorow, 1976).

Are At Least Early Gender Concepts Female Concepts?

The variants of psychoanalytic theories that emphasize the significance of female caretakers in the development of children's gender concepts must predict that female-related cues will be more powerful determinants of preschoolers' gender attribution than male-related cues. The results of the picture experiment might suggest support for this view, but its evidence does not directly address the issue of gender attribution because the real gender of the stimulus figures was indeterminate. Instead, the most satisfactory way to evaluate this prediction is to consider gender attribution when the gender of the stimulus figure was known and the cues were varied, as in the videotape experiments. Neither experiment yielded support: Gender attribution was equally accurate for female- and for male-related cues. In addition, preschool through eight grade children associated approximately the same numbers of traits with most women and with most men in the constituents-of-gender-schema experiment. Overall, as we will argue below, our data suggest that children's gender concepts contain information about both sexes and that they hold concepts for both sexes. Thus, the psychoanalytic theories, both Freud's version and the more recent female-caretaker versions, did not fare well in terms of our data from children, nor did we obtain strong support for the cultural penis model.

Are Gender Concepts Same-Sex Concepts?

Traditional social learning (e.g., Bandura & Walters, 1963; Kagan, 1964; Mischel, 1970) and cognitive-developmental (Kohlberg, 1966) models hypothesize that children learn to imitate same-gender models. So, in fact, do psychoanalytic views. Traditional social learning views propose that this learning occurs through selective reinforcement and imitation, whereas the cognitive model holds that children learn their gender identity, want to be like that gender, and pursue activities, traits, and so forth that they associate with their gender. A recent model of social learning (Perry & Bussey, 1979) also makes the same general predictions but for somewhat different reasons. These authors propose that

> children learn which behaviors are appropriate to each sex by observing differences in the frequencies with which male and female models as groups perform various responses in given situations. Furthermore, children employ these abstractions of what constitutes male-appropriate and female-appropriate behavior as models of their imitative behavior. (p. 1699)

This model assumes that children actively compute or develop a representation of the frequencies with which the two sexes behave in specific ways in given situations. They may then decide to imitate what they detect to be gender-appropriate behavior, particularly if this behavior has led to soccial reward of the models. This latter portion of the model is derived directly from traditional social learning approaches, of course.

In general, these views predict greater sensitivity to same-gender than to other-gender cues, a prediction for which we found no evidence. Williams and Best (1982) also observed no same-gender advantage for a Euro-American sample, nor did Carlsson et al. (1980) with a Swedish sample. In other work, however, Kessler and McKenna (1978) did find some supportive evidence. Finally, Williams, Best, and their associates (Best et al., 1977; Williams et al., 1975) reported that male stereotypes are learned before female ones. Their results may reflect their use of a forced-choice technique which, when coupled with the kind of cultural male bias that we found when subjects had to guess about gender, and the use of older subjects in many cases, could easily explain why their subjects might have been more likely to attribute traits to males.

Do Gender Concepts Depend on Gender Constancy?

Another prediction of the cognitive-developmental model received limited support. According to Kohlberg (1966), gender identity should develop before gender constancy. The gender-identity-before-gender-constancy order appeared in the drawing, picture, and gender constancy experiments, but possession of these concepts did not predict gender attribution in the drawing and picture experiments. Thus, gender attribution and related concepts seem to be independent of, not dependent on, gender identity and gender constancy. Consistent with results of others, we found that gender constancy showed a systematic ordering of knowledge that gender remains constant over time (temporal gender constancy) to precede knowledge that gender remains constant even if one wanted to change it (motivational constancy) and under different situations (situational gender constancy). Nonetheless, when children have experienced the situations themselves, 90% of three- and four-year-olds exhibited situational gender constancy.

What Are Some Sources of Gender Concepts?

All of the above models, with the possible exception of the cultural penis view, suggest that parents will have a major influence on gender concepts. All of the psychoanalytic models stress parental influence, and the others also emphasize the parents, along with others in the child's immediate environment. These models do not deny that teachers, peers, books, and television may play a significant role, but they do not accord these sources as prominent a role as that of the parents. Our data present a different view. The children used hair cues in a highly systematic way regardless of the characteristics of their own hair and their ethnic background. Thus, children with dark, straight, short hair were just as likely to attribute blond, curly, long hair to females as were children with blond, curly, long hair. Children with dark, straight, short hair were as likely to attribute these characteristics to males as were children with other combinations of hair cues. The same situation obtained for white children and for children from minority groups. Because our minority children were Black, Hispanic, and Asian, it seems likely that their relatives had dark hair and brown eyes, just as they had. And yet, they were as likely as white children to identify females as blue-eyed people with long blond, curly hair. These results suggest that factors outside the immediate family must influence the development of cues for gender attribution. As reported in Chapters 4 and 5, books and television seemed to be the most likely candidates. Thoughts of *Goldilocks* led us to examine a sample of 100 children's books for gender-differentiating hair cues. We drew a blank. Goldilocks may have golden locks, but other female main characters were as likely to have dark, straight, short hair as light, curly, long hair. Unfortunately, girls were the main characters in less than half of the books we examined. Boy characters (present in 96% of the books) also showed a full range of hair cues.

Next, we scrutinized children's television programs. This time, our hunch paid off: Both girls and boys were hair-stereotyped in just the ways our subjects had indicated. Even female animals, such as the mother bears, had lighter fur than the males. (Lest any one miss the rather subtle hair cues, the mother animals always wore their signature of femininity, the apron. Little wonder even our preschoolers thought that women cook.) These surveys do not pinpoint television as the only or as a highly significant source of information about gender markers, but, coupled with the surprising potency of hair cues, they strongly imply that extraparental factors may be more important determiners of children's gender concepts than has usually been noted (also see Drabman et al., 1981; Eron et al., 1983; McGhee & Frueh, 1980; Morgan, 1982).

Are Self Concepts The Same As Cultural Gender Concepts?

The gender schema models make interesting, different predictions. All of these models, in addition to the cultural penis model and the others, to a lesser extent, postulate that people develop mental structures that contain gender-relevant information. The gender schema models go further, assuming that the gender schemata function to guide attention and behavior toward gender-related information. Individuals who have minimally developed gender schemata would be less likely to notice gender differences than those with well developed schemata, just as those with minimally developed schemata are less likely to respond in gender-stereotyped ways than are those with well developed gender schemata.

Two of these models focus mainly on adults; the third considers children, as well. Of the adult models, Bem's (1981, 1982) view assumes that sex-typed people (e.g., feminine women and masculine men) are gender-schematic and therefore will show the kind of schema control mentioned above. Women and men with extensive or few traits typically associated with the two sexes will be gender-aschematic and will not manifest the same kind of gender-schema control that the gender-schematic people do. Markus and her associates (Crane & Markus, 1982; Markus et al., 1982) contend that all people are gender-schematic except those who do not claim to have many traits associated with either gender (the undifferentiated). The gender-schematic individuals include the masculine schematics, the feminine schematics, the androgynous (those who claim to possess substantial numbers of both feminine and masculine traits). Note that the masculine and feminine schematics may be of either sex. Martin and Halverson (1981) posit that children develop an ''own-sex'' or ''in-group'' schema before they develop an ''other-sex'' or ''out-group'' one. Before either schema is formulated, the children must be able to accurately identify gender. Without this ability they would not be able to correctly label gender-related information. Thus, Martin and Halverson's approach predicts that gender concepts will be acquired in the following order: gender identity, own-sex schema, other-sex schema. Their model assumes that this order will be a general one; hence, they do not discuss differences between gender schematics and gender aschematics.

Evaluation of these predictions is tricky. The predictions of the Bem and Markus models cannot be compared directly with those of Martin and Halverson, because the former address adult schemata, whereas the latter considers children's schemata, which may be quite different. More important, the models do not distinguish between a schema that includes gender information about one's own self, a schema that includes gender information about others of the same sex, and a schema that includes information about others of the opposite sex. Martin and Halverson's view comes the closest to making these distinctions, but it does not distinguish between schemata for others of each of the two sexes. Unless the references of the schemata are clarified, there is no reasonable way to distinguish a gender schematic from a gender aschematic. To illustrate the problem, we take examples from Bem's definition. If being gender schematic means that a woman believes that she possesses many of the traits typically assigned to women, this meaning differs substantially from one that defines being gender schematic as assigning female-related traits to women on the assumption that women are *de facto* feminine. In the first case, the definition refers to the person's own self descriptions and it says nothing about the person's beliefs about women in general. In the second case, the meaning refers to cultural beliefs about men in general and says nothing about personal gender views. These definitions are very different, of course, so we need to be certain what definition is assumed by a model before it can be evaluated.

Both the Bem and the Markus models apparently entail the self-description view of gender schema, and the Martin-Halverson one assuredly does. Assessments of these gender schemata are derived from self descriptions. But what about schemata for others of either the same or the opposite sex? How do we evaluate these schemata? The standard approach is to obtain assessments of most women, women in general, successful women, and the like. Strictly speaking, this information, intended to describe a large group of people, is of a different order of magnitude than that of self ratings. In the one case, we obtain an estimate of a person's beliefs about self; in the second case, we obtain an estimate of cultural stereotyping. Now suppose a person is gender-schematic in Bem's sense, say a feminine woman. Does this mean that she also believes that most women are feminine? Or does it entail nothing beyond her personal sense of self? If the latter is true, how can she attribute gender or gender-related traits to the other sex? It seems to us that a full analysis of gender schemata requires assessment of beliefs about both the self and about others of both sexes, a practice that has not been employed in the research cited by these investigators.

One way of evaluating these models is to assume that most members of a culture, particularly adult members, share similar gender stereotypes. If so, we can focus on self-ratings. This assumption is questionable, however, as our experiment on the constituents of gender concepts indicated. Although the subjects showed marked agreement at each of the ages tested, the traits on which they agreed changed with the ages tested and, at the preschool and fourth grade levels, did not include the personality traits tested in most experiments. Thus, it seems that both self and cultural gender schemata change with age.

Further evidence comes from a series of studies in our laboratory with college students. We asked these students, both female and male, to describe themselves and to describe most women and most men. The descriptions all involved evaluating traits such as the ones we used in the experiment described in Chapter 7. The general outcome was that self and cultural descriptions often deviated. Although some persons attributed mostly instrumental traits both to themselves and to most others of the same sex, this pattern was unusual. It was far more common for subjects to show substantial differences between their attributions to self and to others even of the same sex. Moreover, the subjects agreed to a much greater extent about cultural stereotypes than they did about their personal attributions. These results convinced us that the two definitions are not synonymous. We conclude that, at present, the gender schema models need clarification before they can be evaluated.

Another problem with evaluating the Martin-Halverson version of a gender schema model is that the other schema may be acquired almost as early as the self schema. Our preschoolers appeared to have not only self schemata, but also some limited ones for most members of their own sex and for most members of the other sex. It may be difficult to ascertain the exact order of acquisition, because children younger than three are not always verbal enough to permit testing.

Overall, the results seem straightforward. Sensitivity to cues about self appear before sensitivity to cues about others (e.g., our data; Eaton & Von Bargen (1981); Wehren & De Lisi, 1983). Then, although the data are somewhat less compelling, sensitivity to cues about same-sex and other-sex people develop at about the same time. The gender schema models do not appear to be sufficiently well developed at this point to handle the data, primarily because they have not formally included distinctions between the individual's awareness of the views of both sexes prevalent in the individual's culture and the extent to which these views have become part of the person's self-concept. People appear to share quite similar ideas about what their culture says about the two sexes; they differ mainly in the extent to which they are incorporating this information into their own personal constructs.

A Revised Cultural Gender Model

What about our cultural gender model? It makes exactly the distinction discussed above. As described in Chapters 1 and 3, we assume that children develop a self concept that may include gender-related components. Simultaneously, they begin to develop concepts for each sex. These schemata will accrue new information and older information will be refined and possibly even deleted as the child matures. We also posited that, with age, children develop a male model against which information is tested.

The results described in Chapter 7 and above strongly support the contention that self and cultural gender concepts develop with age and are not identical. The differences between the self and cultural concepts also were noted by Spence, Helmreich, and Stapp (1975). Specifically, early constituents of cultural concepts include physical cues about hair, eyes, strength, and so forth. Later, information about activities, occupations, and the like are added, followed by personality traits. For self concepts, physical cues also exist, but these are accurate for the person and may deviate from those that are part of the cultural gender concepts. The same is true for the other cues. Thus, this part of the cultural gender model fared reasonably well.

In contrast, the idea of a male protocol encountered difficulties. It suffered the same problems as the cultural penis model. Our subjects, regardless of their ages, appeared to have concepts for both sexes. If they come to use one concept as a model or protocol for evaluating others, this process occurs later than the eighth grade.

To summarize our perspective on the development of gender concepts, we now think that by the time children are three years of age, they have learned their names, the color of their eyes and hair, their gender identity and other descriptive information about themselves that they encode in their self-concept. This self-concept contains some gender-related items. They also are developing gender concepts for the two sexes. At early ages, these items refer to physical characteristics, particularly hair and eye cues, which are used for gender attribution. The gender concepts also contain some other items, gradually including some about activities and occupations, at least. This information is not necessarily accurate, of course, as was demonstrated by the beliefs of youngsters that most women stand while urinating. The gender constancies, which also become part of the concepts, are unrelated to the ability to accurately attribute gender. At a later age, between the fourth and the eighth grade, personality traits enter the gender concepts. The progressive accumulations of these constituents of gender concepts are shown by the increase in gender typing (above-chance attributions of traits to most members of one gender) from preschool through the fourth grade and a decline thereafter and a steady increase in gender stereotyping (differential attributions of the traits to the two genders in accordance with traditional societal expectations) through the eighth grade.

Some Extensions of a Cultural Gender Model

One effect of gender concepts was probed in the experiment reported in Chapter 8. A traditional view of mental health, held by psychoanalytic therapists as well as others, assumes that developing a self-concept that is consistent with the cultural gender concepts for one's sex is important for mental health and adjustment. Thus, girls who know and incorporate expressive characteristics and boys who know and incorporate instrumental characteristics into their self-concepts are likely to be better adjusted than children who deviate from these patterns. In contrast, some contemporary views, including those of Bem (1974), Spence, Helmreich, and Stapp (1975), maintained that having high levels of both instrumental and expressive traits (psychological androgyny) would permit individuals to select behavioral responses that were appropriate to the situation. Hence, the androgynous should be better adjusted than the nonandrogynous. To study these predictions, we had fourth and ninth graders and college students rate well-adjusted and poorly-adjusted peers using instrumental and expressive personality traits. In general, they attributed more expressive and more instrumental traits to the peers they considered well-adjusted than to the peers they considered poorly-adjusted, thus supporting the androgynous, but not the traditional model of gender typing and mental health.

Thus, one application of gender schema and related models is to the relation people expect between certain traits often associated with gender and adjustment. Numerous other applications and implications exist. These include the implication that a nonparental source such as television may influence children's gender concepts as much or more than parents and others in the child's environment.

Another is that children almost certainly will develop gender stereotypes that reflect cultural stereotypes, their own self-concepts do not necessarily contain the same constituents as the cultural stereotypes. What are the factors that govern the extent to which the self-concepts will share features with cultural gender concepts? Not much is known about this issue, despite its importance. Many of my friends, contemporary parents who, like parents throughout the centuries, are trying hard to be excellent parents, are concerned about this issue. Should they be sure to buy trucks and dolls for their daughters and sons alike? How should they handle the gender-stereotyping so prevalent in the media? These are perplexing questions with no ready answers. Remember, for example, that all of the feminists of today (and, presumably, those of days gone by) grew up exposed to gender stereotyped models. Why did they, and not some of their peers, choose self-concepts that are discrepant from their cultural gender concepts?

A final implication of our work is that gender concepts change with age. The last is undoubtedly the most important, for it is through the malleability of the gender concepts that we may be able to modify both personal views and cultural stereotypes about gender.

At this point, I think that it is imperative to step back a bit, to survey the assumptions underlying contemporary approaches to gender roles. In much of this work, scales of traits commonly associated with one sex or the other are used to classify people who rate their own possession of the traits or to classify others in terms of the extent to which they are assigned traits pronounced by the society to be associated with females or males. The effect of these approaches is to perpetuate the view that certain personality and other traits exist that do, in fact, discriminate among the sexes. For many traits, including personality variables, this view is false. That is, the distributions of the two sexes overlap to such an extent that only a small proportion of the variance can be explained on the basis of sex. This result seems to hold for verbal ability, mathematical ability, spatial ability (Hyde, 1981), aggression (Hyde, 1984), and causal attributions for success and failure (Frieze, Whitley, Hanusa, & McHugh, 1982). Sometimes, responses are influenced by the situation and similar factors (Becker, 1986; Eagly & Carli, 1981; Hall & Halberstadt, 1986; Taylor & Hall, 1982). A major primary message to be extracted from much of this work is that the differences are greater within a sex than between the sexes.

And yet, beliefs in gender differences live on even in the face of substantial evidence that few real differences exist. Why? Because gender differences are part of the myth constantly being reiterated by the media, the law, the workplace, and other institutions in our society. This myth also is being perpetuated by researchers' preoccupation with tests of gender roles.

The process of understanding how we learn what gender we are and how this knowledge affects the way in which we perceive ourselves and others is just beginning. In all probability, a comprehensive model will have to be far more complex than the cultural gender model sketched herein. One reason for the added complexity is to explain why, despite the increasing evidence for the similarity of the two genders, people seem determined to dichotomize them (e.g., Deaux, 1976; Rubin et al., 1981). By now, most evidence (e.g., Chapter 7 and Williams & Best, 1982) argues that personality traits and other characteristics of *people* vary continuously not dichotomously. Another reason why more complicated models may be formulated in the future is the need to take situations into account. This need is compatible with the current assumptions that the possession of a wide variety of traits provides one with the flexibility to respond adaptively to a changing environment. We also look forward to the possibility that the concept of sex or gender may lose its "master role," and, in so doing, will enable individuals to be characterized by their own unique combination of characteristics, not by attributions based on their gender.

References

Anderson, R.E. (1966). A computer program for Guttman Scaling with the Good-enough technique. *Behavioral Science, 11,* 235.

Armentrout, J.A., & Burger, G.K. (1972). Children's reports of parental childrearing behavior at five grade levels. *Developmental Psychology, 7,* 44–48.

Ashmore, R.D., & Del Boca, F.K. (1979). Sex stereotypes as implicit personality theory: Toward a cognitive-social psychological conceptualization. *Sex Roles, 5,* 219–248.

Atkin, C. (1985). Effects of television advertising on children: Second year experimental evidence. Michigan State University, Department of Communication.

Bandura, A., & Walters, R. (1963). *Social learning and personality development.* New York: Holt, Rinehart & Winston.

Barclay, C.D., Cutting, J.E., & Kozlowski, L.T. (1978). Temporal and spatial factors in gait perception that influence gender recognition. *Perception & Psychophysics, 23,* 145–152.

Barkley, R.A., Ullman, D.G., Otto, L., & Brecht, J.M. (1977). The effects of sex typing and sex appropriateness of modeled behavior on children's imitation. *Child development, 48,* 721–725.

Baumrind, D. (1982). Are androgynous individuals more effective persons and parents? *Child Development, 53,* 44–75.

Becker, B.J. (1986). Influence again: An examination of reviews and studies of gender difference in social influence. In J.S. Hyde & M.C. Linn (Eds.), *The psychology of gender advances through meta-analysis.* Baltimore, MD: The Johns Hopkins University Press.

Bem, S.L. (1974). The measurement of psychological androgyny. *Journal of Consulting and Clinical Psychology, 42,* 155–162.

Bem, S.L. (1975). Sex role adaptability: One consequence of psychological androgyny. *Journal of Personality and Social Psychology, 31,* 634–643.

Bem, S.L. (1981). Gender schema theory: A cognitive account of sex typing. *Psychological Review, 88,* 354–364.

Bem, S.L. (1982). Gender schema theory and self-schema compared: A comment on Markus, Crane, Bernstein, and Siladi's "Self-Schemas and Gender." *Journal of Personality and Social Psychology, 43,* 1192–1194.

Bem, S.L., & Lenney, E. (1976). Sex typing and the avoidance of cross-sex behavior. *Journal of Personality and Social Psychology, 33,* 48–54.

Best, D.L., Williams, J.E., & Briggs, S.R. (1980). A further analysis of the affective meanings associated with male and female sex-trait stereotypes. *Sex Roles, 6,* 735–746.

Best, D.L., Williams, J.E., Cloud, J.M., Davis, S.W., Robertson, L.S., Edwards, J.R., Giles, H., & Fowles, J. (1977). Development of sex-trait stereotypes among young children in the United States, England, and Ireland. *Child Development, 48,* 1375–1384.

Beuf, A. (1974). Doctor, lawyer, household drudge. *Journal of Communication, 24,* 142–145.

Biller, H.B. (1976). The father and personality development: Paternal deprivation and sex-role development. In M.E. Lamb (Ed.), *The role of the father in child development.* New York: Wiley.

Birdwhistell, R.L. (1970). *Kinesthetics and contexts.* Philadelphia: University of Pennsylvania Press.

Blakemore, J.E.O., LaRue, A.A., & Olejnik, A.B. (1979). Sex-appropriate toy preference and the ability to conceptualize toys as sex-role related. *Developmental Psychology, 15,* 339–340.

Bleier, R. (1987, February). Sex differences research in the neurosciences. American Association for the Advancement of Science Symposium, *Bias in Sex Differences Research,* Chicago.

Bleier, R., Houston, L., & Byne, W. (1986). Can the corpus callosum predict gender, age, handedness, or cognitive differences? *Trends in Neurosciences, 9,* 391–394.

Block J.H. (1978). Another look at sex differentiation in the socialization behaviors of mothers and fathers. In J. Sherman & F. Denmark (Eds.), *Psychology of women: Future directions of research.* New York: Psychology Dimensions.

Brabant, S. (1976). Sex-role stereotyping in the Sunday comics. *Sex Roles, 2,* 231–237.

Brieland, D., & Nelson, L. (1951). Age trends in sex identification as determined by a picture test. *American Psychologist, 6,* 309 (abstract).

Brophy, J.E., & Good, T.L. (1974). *Teacher-student relationships: Causes and consequences.* New York: Holt, Rinehart and Winston.

Buffery, A.W.H., & Gray, J.A. (1972). Sex differences in the development of spatial and linguistic skills. In C. Ounsted and D.C. Taylor (Eds.), *Gender differences: Their ontogeny and significance.* Baltimore, MD: Williams & Wilkins.

Bull, J.J., & Vogt, R.C. (1979). Temperature-dependent sex determination in turtles. *Science, 206,* 1186–1188.

Burger, G.K., Lamp, R.E., & Rogers, D. (1975). Developmental trends in children's perceptions of parental child-rearing behavior. *Developmental Psychology, 11,* 391.

Cann, A., & Haight, J.M. (1983). Children's perceptions of relative competence in sex-typed occupations. *Sex Roles, 9,* 767–773.

Carlsson, M., Andersson, K., Berg, E., & Jaderquist, P. (1980). Sex-role opinions of Swedish children. Uppsala Psychological Reports, No. 289. Department of Psychology, University of Uppsala, Sweden.

Carter, D.B., & Patterson, C.J. (1982). Sex roles as social conventions: The development of children's conceptions of sex-role stereotypes. *Developmental Psychology, 18,* 812–824.

Cassata, M. (1983). The more things change, the more they are the same: An analysis of soap operas from radio to television. In M. Cassata and T. Skill (Eds.), *Life on daytime television: Tuning-in American Serial Drama* (pp. 85–100). Norwood, NJ: Ablex.

Chafetz, J.S. (1974). *Masculine/feminine or human? An overview of the sociology of sex roles.* Itasca, IL: F.E. Peacock.

Cherry, L. (1975). The preschool teacher-child dyad: Sex differences in verbal interactions. *Child Development, 46,* 532–535.

Chi, J.G., Dooling, E.C., & Gilles, F.H. (1977). Gyral development of the human brain. *Annals of Neurology, 1,* 86–93.

Chodorow, N. (1976). Oedipal asymmetries and heterosexual knots. *Social Problems, 23,* 454–468.

Clark, H.H., & Clark, E.V. (1977). *Psychology and language.* New York: Harcourt Brace Jovanovich.

Coker, D.R. (1984). The relationships among gender concepts and cognitive maturity. *Sex Roles, 10,* 19–31.

Conn, J.H. (1940). Children's reactions to the discovery of genital differences. *American Journal of Orthopsychiatry, 10,* 747–755.

Constantinople, A. (1973). Masculinity-femininity: An exception to the famous dictum? *Psychological Bulletin, 80,* 389–407.

Cordua, G.D., McGraw, K.O., & Drabman, R.S. (1979). Doctor or nurse: Children's perceptions of sex-typed occupations. *Child Development, 50,* 590–593.

Costanzo, P.R. (1970). Conformity development as a function of self-blame. *Journal of Personality and Social Psychology, 14,* 366–374.

Courtney, A.E., & Whipple, T.W. (1983). *Sex stereotyping in advertising.* Lexington, MA: Lexington Books.

Crane, M., & Markus, H. (1982). Gender identity: The benefits of a self-schema approach. *Journal of Personality and Social Psychology, 43,* 1195–1197.

Cummings, S., & Taebel, D. (1980). Sexual inequality and the reproduction of consciousness: An analysis of sex-role stereotyping among children. *Sex Roles, 6,* 631–644.

Cunningham, J.C., & Odom, R.D. (1978). The role of perceptual salience in the development of analysis and synthesis processes. *Child Development, 49,* 815–823.

Cutting, J.E., & Kozlowski, L.T. (1977). Recognizing friends by their walk: Gait perception with familiarity cues. *Bulletin of the Psychonomic Society, 9,* 353–356.

Cutting, J.E., Proffitt, D.R., & Kozlowski, L.T. (1978). A biomechanical invariant for gait perception. *Journal of Experimental Psychology: Human Perception and Performance, 4,* 357–372.

David, D.S., & Brannon, R. (1976). *The Forty-nine percent majority.* Reading, MA: Addison-Wesley.

Davis, S.W., Williams, J.E., & Best, D.L. (1982). Sex-trait stereotypes in the self and peer descriptions of third grade children. *Sex Roles, 8,* 315–331.

Deaux, K. (1976). *The behavior of women and men.* Monterey, CA: Brooks/Cole.

Deaux, K. (1982). From individual differences to social categories: Analysis of a decade's research on gender. Presidential address, Midwestern Psychological Association meeting, Chicago, Illinois.

de Lacoste-Utamsing, C., & Holloway, R.L. (1982). Sexual dimorphisms in the human corpus callosum. *Science, 216,* 1431–1432.

Deutsch, C.J., & Gilbert, L.A. (1976). Sex role stereotypes: Effect on perceptions of self and others and on personal adjustment. *Journal of Counseling Psychology, 23,* 373–379.

Deutsch, H. (1944). *The psychology of women.* New York: Grune & Stratton.

Drabman, R.S., Robertson, S.J., Patterson, J.N., Jarvie, G.J., Hammer, D., & Cordua, G. (1981). Children's perceptions of media-portrayed sex roles. *Sex Roles, 7,* 379–389.

Eagly, A.H., & Carli, L.L. (1981). Sex of researchers and sex-typed communications as determinants of sex differences in influenceability: A meta-analysis of social influence studies. *Psychological Bulletin, 90,* 1–20.

Eaton, W.O., & Von Bargen, D. (1981). Asynchronous development of gender understanding in preschool children. *Child Development, 52,* 1020–1027.

Edelbrock, C., & Sugawara, A.I. (1978). Acquisition of sex-typed preferences in preschool-aged children. *Developmental Psychology, 14,* 614–623.

Ehrhardt, A.A., & Meyer-Bahlburg, H.F.L. (1981). Effects of prenatal sex hormones in gender-related behavior. *Science, 211,* 1312–1318.

Emmerich, W., Goldman, K.S., Kirsh, B., & Sharabany, R. (1977). Evidence for a transitional phase in the development of gender constancy. *Child Development, 48,* 930–936.

Erikson, E.H. (1964). Inner and outer space: Reflections on womanhood. In R.J. Lifton (Ed.), *The woman in America.* Boston: Beacon.

Eron, L.D., Huesman, L.R., Brice, P., Fischer, P., & Mermelstein, R. (1983). Age trends in the development of aggression, sextyping, and related television habits. *Developmental Psychology, 19,* 71–77.

Etaugh, C., & Riley, S. (1979). Knowledge of sex stereotyping in preschool children. *Psychological Reports, 44,* 1279–1282.

Fagot, B.I. (1974). Sex differences in toddlers' behavior and parental reaction. *Developmental Psychology, 10,* 554–558.

Fagot, B.I. (1978). The influence of sex of child on parental reactions to toddler children. *Child Development, 49,* 459–465.

Fagot, B.I. (1985). Changes in thinking about early sex role development. *Developmental Review, 5,* 83–98.

Falkender, P.J. (1980). Categorical habituation with sex-typed toy stimuli in older and younger preschoolers. *Child Development, 51,* 515–519.

Farrell, W. (1974). *The liberated man.* New York: Random House.

Fein, G., Johnson, D., Kosson, N., Stork, L., & Wasserman, L. (1975). Sex stereotypes and preferences in the toy choices of 20-month-old boys and girls. *Developmental Psychology, 11,* 527–528.

Flaherty, J.F., & Dusek, J.B. (1980). An investigation of the relationship between psychological androgyny and components of self-concept. *Journal of Personality and Social Psychology, 38,* 984–992.

Flerx, V.C., Fidler, D.S., & Rogers, R.W. (1976). Sex role stereotypes: Developmental aspects of early intervention. *Child Development, 47,* 998–1007.

Freud, S. (1933). Femininity. In J. Strachey (Trans. and Ed.), *New introductory lectures on psychoanalysis.* New York: Norton, 1965.

Freud, S. (1948). Some psychical consequences of the anatomical distinction between the sexes. In J. Riviere (Trans.), *Collected Papers,* Vol. V. London: Hogarth Press.

Frey, K.S., & Ruble, D.N. (1981, April). *Concepts of gender constancy as mediators of behavior.* Paper presented at the biennial meeting of the Society for Research in Child Development, Boston.

Fricke, H.W., & Fricke, S. (1977). Monogamy and sex change by aggressive dominance in coral reef fish. *Nature, 266,* 830–832.

Friedman, L.J. (1977). *Sex role stereotyping in the mass media: An annotated bibliography.* New York: Garland.

Frieze, I., Whitley, B.E., Jr., Hanusa, B.H., & McHugh, M.C. (1982). Assessing the theoretical models for sex differences in causal attributions for success and failure. *Sex Roles, 8,* 333–343.

Frueh, T., & McGhee, P.E. (1975). Traditional sex role development and amount of time spent watching television. *Developmental Psychology, 11,* 109.

Frykholm, G. (1983a). Perceived identity I: Recognition of others by their kinematic patterns. *Uppsala Psychological Reports,* No. 351.

Frykholm, G. (1983b). Perceived identity II: Learning to recognize others by their kinematic patterns. *Uppsala Psychological Reports,* No. 352.

Garrett, C.S., Ein, P.L., & Tremaine, L. (1977). The development of gender stereotyping in adult occupations in elementary school children. *Child Development, 48,* 507–512.

Gazzaniga, M.S., & LeDoux, J.E. (1978). *The integrated mind.* New York: NY: Plenum.

Geschwind, N., & Behan, P. (1982). Left-handedness: Association with immune disease, migraine, and developmental learning disorder. *Proceedings of National Academy of Sciences, 79,* 5097–5100.

Gettys, L.D., & Cann, A. (1981). Children's perceptions of occupational sex stereotypes. *Sex Roles, 7,* 301–308.

Good, T.L., Sikes, J.N., & Brophy, J.E. (1973). Effects of teacher sex and student sex on classroom interaction. *Journal of Educational Psychology, 65,* 74–87.

Goodnow, J.J. (1978). Visible thinking: Cognitive aspects of change in drawings. *Child Development, 49,* 637–641.

Gouze, K.R., & Nadelman, L. (1980). Constancy of gender identity for self and others in children between the ages of three and seven. *Child Development, 51,* 275–278.

Hall, J.A., & Halberstadt, A.G. (1980). Masculinity and femininity in children: Development of the children's personal attributes questionnaire. *Developmental Psychology, 16,* 270–280.

Hall, J.A., & Halberstadt, A.G. (1986). Smiling and gazing. In J.S. Hyde & M.C. Linn (Eds.), *The psychology of gender, advances through Meta-analysis.* Baltimore, MD: The Johns Hopkins Press.

Harshman, R.A., & Remington, R. (1976). *Sex, language and the brain, part I: A review of the literature on adult sex differences in lateralization.* (UCLA Working Papers in Phonetics). Los Angeles: Phonetics Laboratory, University of California, Los Angeles.

Hartley, R.E. (1959). Sex-role pressures and the socialization of the male child. *Psychological Reports, 5,* 457–468.

Haugh, S.S., Hoffman, C.D., & Cowan, G. (1980). The eye of the very young beholder: Sex typing of infants by young children. *Child Development, 51,* 598–600.

Heilbrun, A.B. (1965). An empirical test of the modelling theory of sex-role learning. *Child Development, 36,* 789–799.

Henley, N.M. (1977). *Body politics: Power, sex, and nonverbal communication.* Englewood Cliffs, NJ: Prentice-Hall.

Horney, K. (1926). The flight from womanhood. *International Journal of Psychoanalysis, 7,* 324–39. Also in H. Kelman (Ed.), *Feminine Psychology.* New York: Norton, 1967.

Horney, K. (1932). The dread of woman. Also in H. Kelman (Ed.), *Feminine Psychology.* New York: Norton, 1967.

Huston, A.C. (1983). Sex typing. In P.H. Mussen & E.M. Hetherington (Eds.), *Handbook of child psychology,* Vol. 4, 4th ed. *Socialization, personality, and social behavior.* New York: Wiley.

Huston, A.C. (1985). The development of sex typing: Themes from recent research. *Developmental Review, 5,* 1–17.

Hyde, J.S. (1981). How large are cognitive gender differences? *American Psychologist, 36,* 892–901.

Hyde, J.S. (1984). How large are gender differences in aggression? A developmental meta-analysis. *Developmental Psychology, 20,* 722–736.

Imperato-McGinley, J., Peterson, R.E., Gautier, T., & Sturlo, E. (1979). Androgens and the evolution of male-gender identity among male pseudohermaphrodites with 5-reductase deficiency. *New England Journal of Medicine, 300,* 1233–1237.

Intons-Peterson, M.J. (in press). *Gender concepts of Swedish and American youth.* Hillsdale, NJ: Erlbaum.

Intons-Peterson, M.J., & Reddel, M. (1984). What do people ask about a neonate? *Developmental Psychology, 20,* 358–359.

Johnson, D.D. (1973–1974). Sex differences in reading across cultures. *Reading Research Quarterly, 9,* 67–86.

Johnson, M.M. (1963). Sex role learning in the nuclear family. *Child Development, 34,* 315–333.

Jones, W.H., Chernovetz, M.E.O., & Hansson, R.O. (1978). The enigma of androgyny: Differential implications for males and females? *Journal of Consulting and Clinical Psychology, 46,* 298–313.

Kagan, J. (1964). Acquisition and significance of sex-typing and sex-role identity. In M.L. Hoffman, & L.W. Hoffman (Eds.), *Review of child development research* (Vol. 1). New York: Russell Sage.

Kaplan, A.G. (1979). Clarifying the concept of androgyny: Implications for therapy. *Psychology of Women Quarterly, 3,* 223–230.

Katcher, A. (1955). The discrimination of sex differences by young children. *The Journal of Genetic Psychology, 87,* 131–143.

Kelly, J.A., & Worell, J. (1977). New formulations of sex-role and androgyny: A critical review. *Journal of Consulting and Clinical Psychology, 45,* 1101-1115.

Kessler, S.J., & McKenna, W. (1978). *Gender: An ethnomethodological approach.* New York: Wiley.

Kimball, M.M. (1981). Women and science: A critique of biological theories. *International Journal of Women's Studies, 4,* 318-338.

Kleinke, C.L., & Nicholson, T.A. (1979). Black and white children's awareness of de facto race and sex differences. *Developmental Psychology, 15,* 84-86.

Kohlberg, L. (1966). A cognitive-developmental analysis of children's sex-role concepts and attitudes. In E.E. Maccoby (Ed.), *The development of sex differences.* Stanford, CA: Stanford University Press.

Kozlowski, L.T., & Cutting, J.E. (1977). Recognizing the sex of a walker from a dynamic point-light display. *Perception & Psychophysics, 21,* 575-580.

Kuhn, D., Nash, S.C., & Brucken, L. (1978). Sex-role concepts of two- and three-year-olds. *Child Development, 49,* 445-451.

Lamb, M.E. (1976). The role of the father: An overview. In M.E. Lamb (Ed.), *The role of the father in child development.* New York: Wiley.

Langlois, J.H., & Downs, A.C. (1980). Mothers, fathers, and peers as socialization agents of sex-typed play behaviors in young children. *Child Development, 51,* 1237-1247.

Levin, S.M., Balistrieri, J., & Schukit, M. (1972). The development of sexual discrimination in children. *Journal of Child Psychology and Psychiatry, 13,* 47-53.

Levitin, T.A., & Chananie, J.D. (1972). Responses of female primary school teachers to sex-typed behaviors in male and female children. *Child Development, 43,* 1309-1316.

Levy, J. (1972). Lateral specialization of the human brain: Behavioral manifestation and possible evolutionary basis. In J.A. Giger (Ed.), *The biology of behavior.* Corvallis, OR: Oregon University Press.

Liss, M.B. (1981). Patterns of toy play: An analysis of sex differences. *Sex Roles, 7,* 1143-1150.

Liss, M.B. (Ed.). (1983). *Social and cognitive skills: Sex roles and children's play.* New York: Academic Press.

Lohaus, A., & Trautner, H.M. (in press). Sex-trait stereotypes and their effects on trait attribution to peers. *Archiv fur psychologie.*

Maccoby, E.E., & Jacklin, C.N. (1974). *The psychology of sex differences.* Stanford, CA: Stanford University Press.

Major, B., Carnevale, P., & Deaux, K. (1981). A different perspective on androgyny: Evaluations of masculine and feminine personality characteristics. *Journal of Personality and Social Psychology, 41,* 988-1001.

Marantz, S.A., & Mansfield, A.F. (1977). Maternal equipment and the development of sex-role stereotyping in five- to eleven-year-old girls. *Child Development, 48,* 668-673.

Marcus, D.E., & Overton, W.F. (1978). The development of cognitive gender constancy and sex role preferences. *Child Development, 49,* 434-444.

Markus, H., Crane, M., Bernstein, S., & Siladi, M. (1982). Self schemas and gender. *Journal of Personality and Social Psychology, 42,* 38-50.

Martin, C.L., & Halverson, C.F., Jr. (1981). A schematic processing model of sex typing and stereotyping in children. *Child Development, 52,* 1119–1134.

Martin, C.L., & Halverson, C.F., Jr. (1983). The effects of sex-typing schemas on young children's memory. *Child Development, 54,* 563–574.

Massad, C.M. (1981). Sex role identity and adjustment during adolescence. *Child Development, 52,* 1290–1298.

Masters, J.C., & Wilkinson, A. (1976). Consensual and discriminative stereotypy of sex-type judgments by parents and children. *Child Development, 47,* 208–217.

McArthur, L.Z., & Eisen, S.V. (1976). Achievements of male and female storybook characters as determinants of achievement behavior by boys and girls. *Journal of Personality and Social Psychology, 33,* 467–473.

McConaghy, M.J. (1979). Gender permanence and the genital basis of gender: Stages in the development of constancy of gender identity. *Child Development, 50,* 1223–1226.

McGhee, P.E., & Frueh, T. (1980). Television viewing and the learning of sex-role stereotypes. *Sex Roles 6,* 179–188.

Mead, M. (1963). *Sex and temperament in three primitive societies.* New York: Norton.

Medin, D.L. (1973). Measuring and training dimensional preferences. *Child Development, 44,* 359–362.

Meyer, B. (1980). The development of girls' sex-role attitudes. *Child Development, 51,* 508–514.

Mischel, W. (1966). A social-learning view of sex differences in behavor. In E.E. Maccoby (Ed.), *The development of sex differences.* Stanford, CA: Stanford University Press.

Mischel, W. (1970). Sex typing and socialization. In P.H. Mussen (Ed.), *Carmichael's manual of child psychology.* New York: Wiley.

Money, J., & Ehrhardt, A.A. (1972). *Man & woman, boy & girl.* Baltimore: The Johns Hopkins University Press.

Moore, C.L. (1985). Another psychobiological view of sexual differentiation. *Developmental Review, 5,* 18–55.

Morgan, M. (1982). Television and adolescents' sex role stereotypes: A longitudinal study. *Journal of Personality and Social Psychology, 43,* 947–955.

Morreale, S.J., Ruiz, G.J., Spotila, J.R., & Standora, E.A. (1982). Temperature-dependent sex determination current practices threaten conservation of sea turtles, *Chelonia mydas. Science, 216,* 1245–1247.

Moyer, J.T., & Nakazono, A. (1978). Population structure, reproductive behavior and protogynous hermaphroditism in the angelfish *Centropyge interruptus* at Miyake-jima, Japan. *Japanese Journal of Ichthyology, 25,* 25–39.

Murray, S.R. (1981). Who is that person? Images and roles of black women. In S. Cox (Ed.), *Female psychology: The emerging self* (pp. 113–123). New York: St. Martin's.

Mussen, P.H., & Rutherford, E. (1963). Parent-child relations and parental personality in relation to young children's sex-role preferences. *Child Development, 34,* 589–607.

Nadelman, L. (1974). Sex identity in American children: Memory, knowledge, and preference tests. *Developmental Psychology, 10,* 413–417.

Newcombe, N. (1982). Sex-related differences in spatial ability: Problems and gaps in current approaches. In M. Potegal Ed.), *Spatial abilities: Development and physiological foundations.* New York: Academic Press.

O'Brien, M., Huston, A.C., & Risley, T. (1983). Sex-typed play of toddlers in a day care center. *Journal of Applied Developmental Psychology, 4,* 1–10.

O'Keefe, E.S.C., & Hyde, J.S. (1983). The development of occupational sex-role stereotypes: The effects of gender stability and age. *Sex Roles, 9,* 481–492.

Olson, D. (1970). *Cognitive development: The child's acquisition of diagonality.* New York: Academic Press.

Orlofsky, J.L., & Windle, M.T. (1978). Sex-role orientation, behavioral adaptability, and personal adjustment. *Sex Roles, 4,* 801–811.

Papalia, D.E., & Tennent, S.S. (1975). Vocational aspirations in preschoolers: A manifestation of early sex role stereotyping. *Sex Roles, 1,* 197–199.

Perry, D.G., & Bussey, K. (1979). The social learning theory of sex differences: Imitation is alive and well. *Journal of Personality and Social Psychology, 37,* 1699–1712.

Pitcher, E.G., & Schultz, L.H. (1983). *Boys and girls at play: The development of sex roles.* New York: Praeger.

Pleck, J.H. (1981). *The myth of masculinity.* Cambridge, MA: MIT Press.

Potkay, C.E., Potkay, C.R., Boynton, G.J., & Klingbeil, J.A. (1982). Perceptions of male and female comic strip characters using the adjective generation technique (AGT). *Sex Roles, 8,* 185–200.

Rasmussen, T., & Milner, B. (1977). The role of early left-brain injury in determining lateralization of cerebral speech functions. *Annals of the New York Academy of Sciences, 299,* 355–369.

Reis, H.T., & Wright, S. (1982). Knowledge of sex-role stereotyping in children aged 3 to 5. *Sex Roles, 8,* 1049–1056.

Rogers, L., & Walsh, J. (1982). Shortcomings of the psychomedical research of John Money and coworkers into sex differences in behavior: Social and political implications. *Sex Roles, 8,* 269–281.

Ross, R.M., Losey, G.S., & Diamond, M. (1983). Sex change in a coral-reef fish: Dependence of stimulation and inhibition in relative size. *Science, 221,* 574–575.

Rubin, R.T., Reinisch, J.M., & Haskett, R.F. (1981). Postnatal gonadal steroid effects on human behavior. *Science, 211,* 1318–1324.

Runeson, S., & Frykholm, G. (1983). Kinematic specification of dynamics as an informational basis for person-and-action perception. *Journal of Experimental Psychology: General, 112,* 585–615.

St. Peter, S. (1979). Jack went up the hill...but where was Jill? *Psychology of Women Quarterly, 4,* 256–260.

Schau, C.G., Kahn, L., Diepold, J.H., & Cherry, F. (1980). The relationships of parental expectations and preschool children's verbal sex-typing to their sex-typed toy play behavior. *Child Development, 51,* 266–270.

Sears, R.R., Rau, L., & Alpert, R. (1965). *Identification and child rearing.* Stanford, CA: Stanford University Press.

Seavey, C.A., Katz, P.A., & Zalk, S.R. (1975). Baby X: The effect of gender labels on adult responses to infants. *Sex Roles, 1,* 103–110.

Segalowitz, J.J., Bebout, L.J., & Lederman, J.J. (1979). Lateralization for reading musical chords: Disentangling symbolic, analytic, and phonological aspects of reading. *Brain and Language, 8,* 315–323.

Serbin, L.A., O'Leary, D.K., Kent, R.N., & Tonick, J.J. (1973). A comparison of teacher response to the preacademic and problem behavior of boys and girls. *Child Development, 44,* 796–804.

Sergent, J. (1983). Role of the input in visual hermispheric asymmetries. *Psychological Bulletin, 93,* 481–512.

Shapiro, D.Y. (1980). Serial female sex changes after simultaneous removal of males from social groups of a coral reef fish. *Science, 209,* 1136–1137.

Sherman, J.A. (1978). *Sex-related cognitive differences.* Springfield, IL: Charles C. Thomas.

Silvern, L.E., & Ryan, V.L. (1979). Self-rated adjustment and sex-typing on the Bem sex role inventory: Is masculinity the primary predictor of adjustment. *Sex Roles, 6,* 739–763.

Slaby, R.G., & Frey, K.S. (1975). Development of gender constancy and selective attention in same-sex models. *Child Development, 46,* 849–856.

Smith, L.B. (1983). Development of classification: The use of similarity and dimensional relations. *Journal of Experimental Child Psychology, 36,* 1–29.

Smith, P.K., & Daglish, L. (1977). Sex differences in parent and infant behavior. *Child Development, 48,* 1250–1254.

Snow, M.E., Jacklin, C.N., & Maccoby, E.E. (1983). Sex-of-child differences in father-child interaction at one year of age. *Child Development, 54,* 227–232.

Spence, J.T., & Helmreich, R.L. (1978). *Masculinity & Femininity: Their Psychological Dimensions, Correlates, and Antecedents.* Austin, TX: University of Texas Press.

Spence, J.T., & Helmreich, R.L. (1981). Androgyny versus gender schema: A comment on Bem's Gender Schema Theory. *Psychological Review, 88,* 365–368.

Spence, J.T., Helmreich, R.L., & Stapp, J. (1975). Ratings of self and peers on sex-role attributes and their relation to self-esteem and conceptions of masculinity and femininity. *Journal of Personality and Social Psychology, 32,* 29–39.

Stake, J., & Katz, J.F. (1982). Teacher-pupil relationships in the elementary school classroom: Teacher-gender and pupil-gender differences. *American Educational Research Journal, 19,* 465–476.

Stericker, A., & LeVesconte, S. (1982). Effect of brief training on sex-related differences in visual-spatial skill. *Journal of Personality and Social Psychology, 43,* 1018–1029.

Sternglanz, S.H., & Serbin, L.A. (1974). Sex role stereotyping in children's television programs. *Developmental Psychology, 10,* 710–715.

Tarrier, N., & Gomes, L. (1981). Knowledge of sex-trait stereotypes: Effects of age, sex, and social class on Brazilian children. *Journal of Cross-Cultural Psychology, 12,* 81–93.

Taylor, M.C., & Hall, J.A. (1982). Psychological androgyny: Theories, methods, and conclusions. *Psychological Bulletin, 92,* 347–366.

Thompson, S.K. (1975). Gender labels and early sex role development. *Child Development, 46,* 339–347.

Thompson, S.K., & Bentler, P.M. (1971). The priority of cues in sex discrimination by children and adults. *Developmental Psychology, 5,* 181–185.

Thornburg, K.R., & Weeks, M.O. (1975). Vocational role expectations of five-year-old children and their parents. *Sex Roles, 1,* 395–396.

Trautner, H.M., Sahm, W.B., & Steverman, I. (1983, August). The development of sex-role stereotypes and classificatory skills in children. Paper given at the Seventh Biennial Meetings of the ISSBD in Munich.

Tremaine, L.S., & Schau, C. (1979). Sex-role aspects in the development of children's vocational knowledge. *Journal of Vocational Behavior, 14,* 317–328.

Tremaine, L.S., Schau, C.G., & Busch, J.W. (1982). Children's occupational sex-typing. *Sex Roles, 8,* 691–710.

Tuddenham, R.D., Brooks, J., & Milkovich, L. (1974). Mothers' reports of behavior of ten-year-olds: Relationships with sex, ethnicity, and mother's education. *Developmental Psychology, 10,* 959–995.

Waber, D.P. (1979). Biological substrates of field dependence: Implications of the sex difference. *Psychological Bulletin, 84,* 1076–1087.

Warner, R.R. (1984). Mating behavior and hermaphroditism in coral reef fishes. *American Scientist, 72,* 128–136.

Webster, B. O'C., & Ingram, D. (1972, June). *The comprehension and production of the anaphoric pronouns "he, she, him, her" in normal and linguistically deviant children.* Committee on Linguistics. Paper presented at a symposium on language disorders in children. Stanford University, Stanford, California.

Wehren, A., & De Lisi, R. (1983). The development of gender understanding: Judgments and explanations. *Child Development, 54,* 1568–1578.

Weitzman, L., Eifler, D., Hokada, E., & Ross, C. (1972). Sex-role socialization in picture books for preschool children. *American Journal of Sociology, 77,* 1125–1150.

Wells, G. (1985). *Language development in the pre-school years.* Cambridge: Cambridge University Press.

Williams, J.E., Bennett, S.M., & Best, D.L. (1975). Awareness and expression of sex stereotypes in young children. *Developmental Psychology, 11,* 635–642.

Williams, J.E., & Best, D.L. (1977). Sex stereotypes and trait favorability on the Adjective Check List. *Educational and Psychological Measurement, 37,* 101–110.

Williams, J.E., & Best, D.L. (1982). *Measuring sex stereotypes: A thirty-nation study.* Beverly Hills, California: Sage.

Williams, J.E., & Morland, J.K. (1987). *Race, Color, and the Young Child.* Chapel Hill, NC: University of North Carolina Press.

Zaknoen, M. (1983). Gender-role identity and adjustment. Unpublished honors thesis, Indiana University, Bloomington.

Author Index

177

Subject Index